THE SAMURAI HUSBAND

RESTORING THE **HONOR** OF A **CHRIST-CENTERED** MARRIAGE

MATT ULRICH

Table of Contents

Introduction

DON'T MISS THIS OR YOU WILL MISS EVERYTHING!

One of the highlights of my early teenage years was going to theme parks with my friends. I absolutely loved the thrill of running past the ticket counter and into the heart of Universal Studios, where for two minutes I was absolutely overwhelmed by the options and the excited uncertainty of where to begin. The choices were endless but in my mind the most important thing was to ensure that I rode all of the fast paced, gut wrenching roller coasters. I loved the feeling of having my stomach in my throat and my equilibrium shot as I staggered off a ride. The hour-long line that I had to stand in before the three minutes of actually coasting, however, was grueling.

There is one line that I waited in that I will never, ever forget. I was waiting in line for the Hulk, one of the most popular roller coasters at Universal Studios in Orlando, Florida at the time... which means the wait was a solid hour in line. There was an old couple waiting in line a few people in front of me and when I say old, I mean they were old. They must have been *at least* in their early 70s. They were constantly holding hands, laughing together, and always seemed to have to be touching one another, even if it was just the wife holding one of her husband's fingers. As I was making small talk with my friends and talking about who was going to puke first as thirteen-year-old boys do, something in front of me caught my eye. I turned around to see that same, cute old couple just going at it. They were making out like they were high schoolers in the closet playing seven minutes in heaven with only fifteen seconds left. I was almost sick before we even rode our first roller coaster! I had never seen anyone over the age of 40 French kissing until that unforgettable day. As a teenage boy, I was absolutely *appalled*.

Now as a married man, I look back at that seemingly traumatic experience and am highly encouraged by what I saw. In fact, that old man has become one of my heroes! I want to be the guy in his 70s who still makes out with his wife. (Because let's face it, if you are making out at 70, you are obviously doing something right!)

But this book isn't about the ten secrets to spice up your love life or some kind of awkward elderly romance novel; it is about building a Biblical foundation for your marriage that is going to help your marriage last until you are 70, 80, or 100. (The making out is up to you.)

I am utterly convinced that the key to a successful, lasting marriage is a proper understanding of God's plan for marriage. Even more importantly, especially for men, it is having a Biblical understanding of what it means to be a husband. How to be a godly husband is becoming a lost art. Men are looking less at the Bible and more at culture and the media to figure out what it means to be a man, a husband, and a father and it is destroying marriages and families at an unprecedented rate. Marriages are a lot more volatile, ending way too often in divorce, and are more frustrating and less fulfilling than God ever intended them to be... because we are taking our cues from the wrong sources! *But the good news is that they don't have to be that way.*

Maybe you have been married for a long time and you are staying together, but have more or less given up on making your marriage work. You have simply settled. Or you might be in the first few years of marriage and thinking to yourself, "This is not what I thought marriage would be like." You may have a few kids and are 10 years into marriage and having a hard time just making it to tomorrow, not realizing that the bride of your youth is ever so slowly but definitely moving in a different direction than you are. You may simply be preparing for marriage and trying to get it right before you even begin! Or you know what, you may just be reading this to expand your repertoire because you are already a stellar husband!

Wherever you are coming from and whatever your case, I have good news for you my friend. I have got the answers. I would even be so bold as to say I have the answers to your specific problems and know exactly how to fix your marriage. If it is already going well, then I have some ideas and things you can do to make it even better. Trust me on this one.

"Why so confident?" you may ask. Because I have a fail-proof plan that is never wrong. I have found a resource that is not only fail-proof but fool-proof, as well. It has been around awhile and has gained some clout throughout the years. Some people hate it, other people love it. Some people swear by it. You may have heard of it.

It is called the Bible.

Here's the thing: I am becoming more and more certain that if you live according to Biblical principles and deeply abide in the presence of Jesus, your life *will get better*. Period. If you are already a follower of Jesus, then you are by default in agreement with my claim. The Bible shows us the best way to live and what is says about marriage and being a husband is absolutely no different. This is what I am banking on in this book: if you apply the principles laid out in Ephesians 5:21-33 faithfully and with all of your heart, soul, mind and strength, your marriage will drastically improve regardless of where it may currently be. The way you view your marriage, how your wife responds to you physically, emotionally, and spiritually, the kind of husband that you are, and most importantly, the glory God is getting from your marriage, *will change for the better*. Now it may take some rewiring of your brain, spirit, and habits. It is going to stretch and challenge how you view yourself, what it means to be a husband and what it means for your wife to be your wife, but I stand by my promise: put this into practice and things will change for the better. This is not an overnight fix, and it will not be easy, but please trust me; it will be worth it.

So before we go any farther, I want you to read the passage that is the bedrock for everything we are going to discuss from here on out: Ephesians 5:21-33.

Submit to one another out of reverence for Christ.

Wives, submit to your husbands as to the Lord. For the husband is the head of the wife as Christ is the head of the church, his body, of which he is the Savior. Now as the church submits to Christ, so also wives should submit to their husbands in everything.

Husbands, love your wives, just as Christ loved the church and gave himself up for her to make her holy, cleansing her by the washing with water through the word, and to present her to himself as a radiant church, without stain or wrinkle or any other blemish, but holy and blameless. In this same way, husbands ought to love their wives as their own bodies. He who loves his wife loves himself. After all, no one ever hated his own body, but he feeds and cares for it, just as Christ does the church— for we are members of his body. "For this reason a man will leave his father and mother and be united to his wife, and the two will become one flesh." This is a profound mystery—but I am talking about Christ and the church. However, each one of you also must love his wife as he loves himself, and the wife must respect her husband.

Now that you have read it, go ahead and read it again. But don't just read; study it. Don't just study it; memorize it. Don't just memorize it; hide it in your heart. Write it up on your bathroom mirror, put it on your steering wheel, tape it to your desk in the office or wherever you are going to see this passage on a daily basis. The Word of God is living and active, so let it do its work! If you put the Word in front of you and meditate on it regularly, you *will* be transformed.

So let the transformation begin…

1

MARRIAGE ISN'T ABOUT WHAT YOU THINK IT IS ABOUT.

From Happy to Holy to Glory

Submit to one another out of reverence for Christ.
- Ephesians 5:21, NIV

I love watching five-year-olds play soccer. You can basically stereotype the entire league into four types of players:

1. **The kickers**: These kids really don't care which way or why, but they are going to hone in on the ball and try to kick it as hard as their little five-year-old body can muster. After making contact they will be sure to scan the

crowd, find their parent and make sure they saw what just happened.

2. **The herd**: These are the kids that just run where the other kids are, not even aware there is a ball to be kicked or that they are playing a team sport.

3. **The criers**: These children are constantly bawling and trying to run to their mom on the sideline while the father is trying to turn them around and point them back to the herd.

4. And finally there are **the hippies**: These kids have no interest whatsoever in soccer but his/her parent wanted them to at least try out a sport. He/she is on the field chasing after a butterfly unaware of the fact that the rest of the kids are down on the other side of the field trying to kick a ball into the goals.

These games are fascinating and so much fun to watch because I would say 80% of the kids don't even know or realize there are rules for playing soccer! They just love running around after the ball. Sure, if you asked them they would say they are playing soccer, but they have no conceptual notion of the game or what is really going on. There is no competitive edge in any of them because honestly, they don't even know what the overarching purpose of the game is. You rarely ever see five years old running off the field asking what the score was because they want to win. They may ask if they won, but you could really tell them anything and they will believe you. You can tell your child that both teams won and they would be ecstatic!

Now say that to a World Cup player and they would look at you like you are crazy, because they don't play for fun... they play to win. A lot is on the line: their professional careers, their country's honor, and the desire to be the absolute best in the world. The simple fact is you can't really win at soccer *if you don't even know what a win looks like.*

Now I want you to do me a favor: go grab your Bible. Open it up to Ephesians 5 and look specifically for verse 21. Where does your translation put that verse? Is it the tail end of Paul's encouragement to be imitators of God in verses 1-20? Or does it put verse 21 as the beginning verse in his exhortation to husbands and wives? Depending on the translation, you have about a 50/50 shot of which section the translator thought that verse belonged.

Why even bring this up? Because which section you think that verse 21 should be in has huge implications for how we view what Paul is about to write to husbands and wives. It's an absolute game changer. "Submit to one another out of reverence for Christ." This verse plays a critical part in framing the rest of what Paul is about to say. If you haven't guessed already, I am convinced that this should not be ignored when referring to the following verse and is supposed to be read in light of Ephesians 5:22-33.

Now this is a loaded little verse we have here. Submit to… one another? Interesting, right? You may be thinking to yourself, "I thought submission was the wife's job." It is, but it isn't hers alone. The kicker here is the latter part of this verse: out of reverence for Christ. This is the reason for marriage in its entirety, summed up in five words. We are to revere Christ in our marriage. He is to be lifted up, glorified, and pointed to through the way a husband and a wife love and interact with each other. If this isn't the root and reason for your marriage or you aren't willing to start moving in that direction, you might as well start chasing butterflies on the soccer field because you have missed the entire point of the game!

From Happy to Holy to Glory

Have you ever asked people what they think the purpose of marriage is? You may be surprised at what kind of answers you get. Look it up on a Google search and you find all kinds of answers: "tax breaks," "to raise a family," "stability," and "to keep divorce attorneys making triple digits," are just a few of the answers you will actually find! One (legitimate) survey done by the Pew Research Center polled over 2,000 randomly selected participants in the United States and asked them a series of questions about marriage. Do you know the #1 answer these randomly selected people gave when they were asked about the purpose of marriage? When asking the non-church attending population, 68% of them said that the main purpose of marriage was for mutual happiness, and a distant second, with 21% said raising children.

Now when Pew researchers talked to those who attended church on a weekly basis, the numbers changed... but not by much! 58% of weekly church attendees said that mutual happiness was the main reason for marriage, while 25% said the main purpose was for raising children. Only 14% said that neither one of these was the main reason for marriage. [1]

What does this mean? It means that the prevailing train of thought for both Christians and non-Christians is that *happiness is paramount in marriage.* That is what the population at large thinks is the main reason and purpose behind why we get hitched. While this may be the prevailing answer that most Americans agree on, it is a far cry from the Biblical idea of marriage, and herein lies a huge problem when it comes to the covenant of marriage. Americans say happiness is paramount; the Bible says that God's glory is the reason for marriage.

So here is the truth of the matter: *Marriage is not about your happiness; it is about God's glory.*

Before I got married, I went on a quest to seek the most godly, experienced counsel on marriage that I could possibly find. I come from a divorced home and that was really rough on my brothers and me, so I resolved to do

---

1 http://pewresearch.org/assets/social/pdf/Marriage.pdf It is interesting because this link is no longer available. It was a few years ago but has been taken off the pewresearch.org website. Why you may ask? *Because questions like this aren't even being asked anymore.* They have been replaced with surveys like "What are the advantages of marriage?" and whether or not the American people even continue to support the idea of marriage: http://www.pewsocialtrends. org/2014/09/24/chapter-1-public-views-on-marriage/

everything I could to ensure that did not happen to my up-and-coming family. I thought taking some preventative measures would pay off some long-term dividends, and boy was I right.

So I set out with a mission of asking anyone and everyone that had been married for over 20 years what their marital advice was for a rookie husband to be. I ended up getting a lot of good words of wisdom, ranging from "Always open the door for your wife no matter how old you get" to, "A happy wife is a happy life!" to, "Have sex as often as possible." (Needless to say, that last one was a favorite of mine!) But there was one person who did not give me any advice, even though I specifically asked for it. I don't even think you could call what he told me wisdom, because it was bigger than that. What he told me actually changed my whole perception on what marriage is and what it is supposed to be about. What he said hit me like a ton of bricks. Even after reading Ephesians 5 for what seemed like a billion times, I had somehow missed this crucial, paradigm shifting thought.

When I asked him for advice, he simply said, "Marriage is not about your happiness. It is about your holiness." I looked at him dumbfounded, because I couldn't even process what he said in that moment. Sure, I nodded my head like I understood, but let's be honest, there are many times we just nod our heads in agreement because we don't want to look stupid, but we really don't get what the person we are talking to just said. Come on, confess, you've done that too.

After walking away from this conversation, the idea that marriage was not about happiness but about my holiness continued to scramble my brain. What does that even mean? How does holiness play a part in marriage? How do I get sanctified by some other person? Wasn't that Jesus' job? Then after some more thought and prayer, things started clicking. The pieces of Ephesians 5 started to resurface. Submit to one another *out of reverence for Christ.* I started meditating on that. What does it mean to revere Christ? It means to be in awe of, to regard with deep admiration and respect, to worship. So my marriage is supposed to simultaneously draw from my relationship and reverence for Christ while at the same time somehow make me admire Christ more, to draw me closer to Him, to actually *increase* my worship of Him. Now if you have been married for any amount of time, you know there are days when marriage may *test* your faith, but to increase your faith and reverence? To actually make you more holy?

I tried breaking this down logically so I could get a better mental and spiritual grip on it. If my wife and I are submitting to one another out of reverence for Christ and it is in turn drawing me closer to Jesus, then I am going to become more holy. If I am "not feeling it" in my marriage, then I am supposed to love my wife anyway out of reverence for Christ, which will in turn also move me towards holiness. I started to get it on the theoretical level, but then thought to myself, what about the day-to-day practical stuff? Sure that sounds nice conceptually speaking, but when you just get home from an insane day at work and all you want to do is crash on the couch but the kids are screaming and hungry, the house is trashed, your wife is stressed, the dishes are not done and the pot of angel hair pasta is bubbling over because your wife got sidetracked changing a blow-out diaper... where does the whole holiness thing come into play?

Now I don't want you to miss this. I even started a new paragraph just so you would pay more attention. *These* are the moments that play an integral role in defining who you are as a husband. These are the types of daily scenarios where God is giving you the opportunity to grow in holiness and Christ likeness. What would make you happy? Letting your wife handle the kids and dinner because hey, you work 50+ hours to provide for this family. The least your wife can do is get the kids under control and put dinner on the table, right? Sure, that might make you happy, but what your wife brings to your marriage and whether you are happy or not aren't even the right questions to be asking. That is like asking how many touchdowns a Red Sox pitcher threw in last night's game versus the Yankees. It's the wrong question entirely... it doesn't even make sense! Touchdowns have nothing to do with baseball.

Likewise, in the context of marriage, you have to start by asking the right question. The question frames everything else and if the question is off, everything else is off from the get go. You can't have the right answer if you don't even have the right question.

The *right* question to be asking yourself in these situations is, "What response is going to draw me closer to Christ, help me to become more like Him, and ultimately give Him the most glory?" When God's glory in your end goal, then holiness always manifests. Trust me, there are going to be days when you are exhausted after a long day's work and you step over that threshold into a house of chaos. The *last* thing you want to do is more work! As a husband, however, you can make the choice to roll up your sleeves, get those dishes done, not only strain the noodles but also throw the sauce on the other burner and give your wife a hand. Yes, you are going to go against what your body, nature, and culture are telling you to do, but you are also choosing to do what you know is the godly thing to do.[2] You tell me which scenario is going to draw you closer to Christ; being the servant or acting like the king and expecting everyone in the household to serve you?

Remember Who You Serve

You remember those WWJD bracelets? Well, I am not saying go out and buy one, but burn that into your mind and make that your mantra when it comes to making decisions as a husband. Just remember: it's not about you. It was never about you. It was never meant to be about you. That simple shift will revolutionize the way you view your marriage and role in it. Jesus was not just the king,

---

2 Matthew 10:39

He was the servant king. He did not come to be served, but to serve and give His life.[3] That is the call of a husband to his wife. *It's not about you.*

The crazy thing is that it isn't about your wife, either. That is where a lot of people who start on the right track derail. It is all about Jesus. We don't lose our rights so our wives can be lifted up. We don't sacrifice so ultimately she can live lavishly or lazily while we slave away serving her. We do so because we are submitting out of reverence for Christ. As husbands, we need to remember who we serve. We serve and love our wives because in doing so, we are serving and loving Jesus. That is the critical connection piece. If your love and sacrifice for your wife is not directly flowing out of your love for the Lord and through His power[4], then that wick is going to burn quickly and you are going to be left with a lot of frustration and contempt at how unfair your marriage has become.

Even though marriage is about your holiness, the ultimate goal of a marriage is for God's glory. The marriage covenant between a man and a woman is supposed to reflect the covenant of Jesus and His bride, the church.

---

3 Matthew 20:28
4 2 Peter 1:3

You as the husband are supposed to embody and represent the fullness of Jesus' love and commitment to the church. For better or for worse... that was your commission to become a living, breathing parable of Jesus' love for His church. A great goal and vision for every husband is to strive to have a relationship with your wife so that if people followed you around for a week, they would say, "So *that* is how Jesus loves me. I get it now. I want Jesus if that is what His love looks like." And once you start loving her in that way, you pave the way for her to start submitting to you as the church submits to Christ.

Turn to Appendix A for some questions to help you dig deeper into the content of this chapter

2

THE DIRTY WORD NO WOMAN WANTS TO HEAR.

S#*%it

Wives, understand and support your husbands in ways that show your support for Christ. The husband provides leadership to his wife the way Christ does to his church, not by domineering but by cherishing. So just as the church submits to Christ as he exercises such leadership, wives should likewise submit to their husbands. –Ephesians 5:22-24, The Message

Talk Dirty to Me!

Women are turned off by the word submission. In fact, most women hate it. It is a taboo topic and a dirty word to say nowadays because of the massive negative connotation it brings. When asked what they think about when they hear the word submission, especially if you ask them in terms of what it means in the Bible when talking about marriage, the majority of women cringe. When I poll women and ask what they think submission means in the context of a marriage, I usually get two answers: they think these verses are either used by men as a way to subjugate and control women under a religious guise of holiness or they genuinely feel that these verses point to the fact that a godly woman in a Christian relationship functionally loses her right to think independently and must always do what her husband says. The sad thing is that these two prevailing thoughts from both in and out of the church regarding what Biblical submission means are just flat-out wrong interpretations of these verses. But if they are so wrong, why are they the popular understandings of what these verses mean?

Just Give Her a Reason

It is amazing what we men will do for the things we love and are passionate about. I had a friend who was a wrestler in high school and he took wrestling very seriously. He needed to drop a few pounds to make a lower weight class so he took drastic measures to make it happen. He dressed himself in a garbage bag and ran around his neighborhood in the scorching heat. He then went up into the attic (still donning his fashionable California raisin-esque garbage bag suit) and starting doing jumping jacks in the 110 degree sweltering heat. (He was either extremely committed or just plain crazy!)

Or what about the Green Bay Packers' football fans? I always had respect for the intensity of Packer fans who are in their forties and fifties and have one of the letters of G-R-E-E-N B-A-Y written on their shirtless pot bellies in the snow and sub-freezing temperatures. Being from Florida, I just don't get it. They don't even look cold! Whether they are somehow staying warm or just freezing and not showing it, one thing is for sure: the Green Bay Packers have some dedicated fans!

In terms of commitment and passion, however, I don't think there is anyone I have met that is more committed to a sport or a team than Boston Red Sox fans. Right after I graduated from college in 2004, I spent eight weeks in Boston with my older brother who was attending Berkeley School of Music at the time. It was my first time to visit Boston and one of the things that I desperately wanted to do was go to a Red Sox game. I am not even a big baseball fan, but my brother lived just a few blocks from Fenway Park and it was in the middle of the baseball season. I would be sitting in his apartment and I could hear the roar of the crowd after what seemed like every play. The noise and buzz of the stadium was like a siren calling to me... I *had* to go check it out. So one day I went to Fenway to buy us tickets. I had to sit outside the stadium for two hours just to get two tickets in a standing-room-only section behind the right field fence. Mind you, all this is definitely *before* their 2004 World Series win, so we are talking about fans who have not seen their team win the World Series in over half a century. Even after the curse of the Bambino had haunted Fenway for decades, you still had to wait in line for two hours just to stand in right field to watch the game!

Once I was in the stadium, the thing that impressed me the most wasn't the Green Monster or the nostalgia of being in one of the most iconic stadiums in America. The thing that impressed me the most came from my incessant eavesdropping on Red Sox fans as my brother and I watched the game. These guys knew *every stat of every player.* From the starters to the bench warmers, you might have thought I was sitting in the players' family section by the way they knew the players' statistics inside and out. These guys were devout followers of the Red Sox. I was so impressed that from that day on, I declared myself a Red Sox fan, even though I don't really watch baseball, because I thought to myself, "If these fans are that committed even though their team hasn't won in *decades,* then I will cast my lot with them!" I am a big loyalty guy, so their tenacity and passion to see their team win and support them through thick and thin won my heart over.

This just goes to show that men have a way of becoming insanely passionate about the things they love. Whether it is any of the sports fanatics listed above, a deer hunter who is willing to sit in a deer stand for 8 hours a day covered in deer pee just to take one shot at a doe during that time, a man who watches seven hours of sports every weekend, or a man who spends $15,000 on a single remote control airplane… men will do some crazy stuff for the things they love.

But when it comes to loving his spouse, the person he committed to spending the rest of his life with in a covenant that is supposed to glorify and point to Jesus, some men have a hard time choosing her over the trivial sports and hobbies they love. Why is that?

Or do you ever wonder why your wife doesn't submit to you the way you want her to or think she should? Let's be honest: it is probably because you haven't given her a reason to. You can't be selfish and do all the things you want to do, watch all the sports or do all the hunting you want and then expect your wife to wait on you hand and foot. If you aren't submitting to and serving your wife, then you really can't blame her for following the leader of the household and reproducing your actions towards her. Don't take my word for it, though. Let's take it back to the Bible and see how this art of submission is supposed to happen. Ephesians 5:21-24 says this:

Submit to one another out of reverence for Christ. Wives, submit to your husbands as to the Lord. For the husband is the head of the wife as Christ is the head of the church, his body, of which he is the Savior. Now as the church submits to Christ, so also wives should submit to their husbands in everything.

Since we have already talked about verse 21, let's dive into verses 22-24 because two very important martial truths come out of these three verses. The first is that your wife should submit to you as she submits to the Lord. Yes, it is true: wives are supposed to submit to their husbands... as unto the Lord. So let me ask you this; why does your wife (or you or anyone for that matter) submit to the Lord? Now you could give a lot of answers that are theologically and doctrinally correct, such as, "Because he is King, Savior, and Lord!" and these would be excellent answers because they are all very true. But I want to propose another reason why we submit to the Lord: *because we know it is the best thing for us.* There have been many times throughout history and even today when people submit to kings, monarchs, and even those who call themselves lords. There are also many times that people flat out rebel against anyone who gives themselves these titles. As I am writing this, there are countries all over the world in protest of their leaders and so-called kings. Why? Because the people do not believe that their leaders have their best interest in mind.

Jesus most certainly holds the key to eternal life in His hand and feely gives it to anyone who desires Him. He has conquered death, hell, and the grave and has resurrected victoriously, allowing access to the Father for all who cry out to Him and that most certainly is enough reason to submit to Him. There is a verse, however, that takes this understanding of why we submit to Him to the next level.

John 17:3 says, "This is eternal life: that they may know you, the one true God, and Jesus Christ whom you sent." Notice that the verse doesn't say, "This is eternal life – that one day you will get to heaven." No, the verse explicitly states that eternal life *is knowing Jesus*. That means that we have access to eternal life right now, as we are living here on earth. Now follow me here – if eternal life is accessible to us now, as we are living and breathing here on earth, then don't you think this is absolutely amazing news? The Kingdom of God, what we are designed and created for, is available for us to experience right now!!

Certainly we submit to the Lord because He is just that, the Lord, but we also submit to Him because we know that when we do we are going to live the most fulfilling life that is possible.[5] Now I am not talking about the American dream of getting every materialistic thing we want and becoming the CEO of your company and garnering

---

5 Psalm 16:11

worldly success. I am talking about following Jesus in a way that satisfies the deepest desires of your soul and spirit. We submit to Jesus because we know that He wants us to experience the absolute best life possible... eternal life here on earth. I know that when I follow Jesus, He has the best in mind for me and will never lead me astray or in the wrong direction. When I submit to Jesus, eternal life and utter fulfillment naturally flow from that relationship.

For the husband is the head of the wife as Christ is the head of the church, his body, of which he is the Savior.

So what, then, is Biblical submission then? What does it look like? When does it start naturally taking place? The second important truth we can glean from this set of verses is that submission begins when a husband loves his wife like Jesus loves the church; passionately, protectively, with her best interest in mind, and all the while expecting nothing in return. When this becomes the husband's default setting, then his wife will feel comfortable and confident in submitting to him. When a wife can feel completely at peace, protected, and utterly confident that her husband would never do anything without thinking of her first and filtering his decisions through how this would affect her, their relationship, and their family, then she will be ready to gladly and joyfully submit. If she thinks she has to compete with football, fishing, your ministry, or your job, then she is going to be more willing to take action on her own apart from what you say is best.

This type of trust and confidence in a husband, however, comes over time. This does not happen overnight, in a week, or even a month. This happens when a husband commits to loving his wife like Jesus loved the church for the rest of his life regardless of how she is going to respond to him. Usually, submission comes after a long string of events and many decisions where you, the husband, prove to your wife that you truly do love her and have her best interest in mind. This kind of trust is garnered when you have the opportunity, for example, to go watch football with the boys but choose to spend time with your wife, instead. Now don't get me wrong: going to watch football with the boys or whatever your pastime may be, is not inherently bad, but when that is chosen over your wife again and again and again, it becomes a point of contention, especially in regards to submission.

Another seemingly obvious but often neglected way to reassure and reaffirm your love to your wife is by stopping what you are doing, looking her in the eyes, and telling her *every single day* that you love her, that she is the most important person in your life, and that you would do anything for her. Her trust in your leadership also accrues when you start finding ways to serve her in the little things, like stopping what you are doing when your wife is walking into the house loaded down with groceries and telling her to go sit down and relax while you unload them for her. I don't know all the nuances of your daily routine, but I can tell you this: the biggest victories in being a husband worth following are won by making the *daily* decisions to serve and love your wife in little ways that you know she appreciates and values.

A Point is a Point

Babe Ruth is a legend. He has hit more home runs than anyone else in history behind Hank Aaron and Barry Bonds (I still have beef with Bonds for using steroids). All three players are notorious for slamming balls out of the park... but they are just as notorious for striking out. They are 1, 2, and 3 all-time for HRs, but are also ranked 44, 87, and 104 as all time strikeout leaders. **Fact**: When you swing for the fences all the time, you are going to strike out more often. Anyone who plays baseball knows that a player who can *consistently* get on base is better for the team than a player who hits the *occasional* home run. The same principle is true in marriage: a husband that intentionally makes small, daily deposits in his marriage does more for his marriage than the husband who sweeps his wife off her feet with epically romantic getaways twice a year... yet neglects the day to day investments.

You see, men remember the big moments. These are the stories that get told again and again to our buddies when we hang out: that time you caught the gigantic fish or when you and your friends won the football championship that year in high school. These are the memories that lodge themselves in our long-term memory and the ones we go back to again and again... and again. Men just don't remember (or care to remember) minutia. We don't care about what happened if it was not something awesome. In fact, this is where men get into a lot of trouble. Example: You think you are being a good husband by relaying the fact to your wife that your best friend and his wife just had a baby. But then your wife drills you for details: boy or a girl? Is the baby healthy? How is the wife feeling? How much did the baby weigh? Was the mom able to hold the baby right away? Did the baby latch on quickly? These, among others, are a bunch of details you could care less about and don't remember (or didn't even bother to ask). Why? Not because you don't *care*... it is just that your brain doesn't work that way. We remember the big and important things: your friend had a baby. Period. What more do you need to know?!

But women's brains are different. Very different.

Most men will go all out for their wives three times a year: her birthday, their anniversary, and Christmas. And a lot of husbands pull out all the stops for these important days of the year thinking that they have covered all their bases and racked up enough points to get them through the rest of the year. In the husband's mind, these netted him at least 33 points each with his wife, giving him an annual score of 99/100 and the feeling of accomplishment and victory. Yet what most husbands fail to realize is that on their wife's scorecard, each of those elaborate outings or gifts only count for one point. Just. One. Point. Which sounds like a bummer, but proves the argument I am trying to make because you know what else counts as one point? You changing the baby's diaper when you weren't asked. Taking out the garbage gets you a point. Brushing your wife's hair or giving her a quick shoulder massage when she didn't ask gets you one point. Doing a load of laundry gets you one point. Randomly telling your wife she is beautiful gets you a point. And the list of small but meaningful tasks and gestures goes on and on.

So don't put your stock in the three big events of the year; accrue your massive amount of points with the small, daily victories of serving and loving your wife well. (Now don't get me wrong; go all out every now and then! Just don't let that be the *only* thing you do!) And if you don't know what those things are that you can do on a daily basis, just ask. Too many husbands waste so much time trying to figure out what their wife wants instead of just asking her what would make her happy! So cut the drama out of the equation and ask your wife how you can love her well this week. Instead of trying to figure her out, getting it wrong, and then getting angry because your wife is impossible to please, *just ask her*! Swallow your pride and save yourself a ton of grief! I try to ask my wife regularly "Am I loving you the way you need to be loved?" This is one of the best decisions I have made and has been extremely helpful with opening up our lines of communication.

Now some of you may be reading this and say, "So I just slave away and let my wife boss me around and do whatever she wants as I pick up after her?" Hardly. Is that was Jesus did? Did the church boss Him around and tell Him what to do? Not even a chance. It really boils down to what you think it means to be a man and what is means to lead well, Biblically speaking. Our culture says that being a man and being a leader means that we are in control and ruling with an iron fist, telling our wives what to do and when to do it. But this is not the way of Jesus. Philippians 2:6-8 says He ruled by example and by leading in a radically selfless way. This did not diminish His authority; this did not embolden His followers to rebel because they saw Him as weak. In fact, it did the opposite. It was endearing and refreshing to see someone in authority not lord it over them[6] and it did nothing but strengthen Jesus' position in this new, counter-cultural way of living and leading. He did not win humanity over with power or might; He did so with love.[7]

---

6 Luke 22:25-26
7 John 15:13

Submitting When It Counts

Here is the good news: if you love your wife well, she will *desire* to submit to you because she knows you have her best interest in mind. If you really love your wife well (and in a way that she receives it) and she knows that you are seeking Jesus, you make decisions together, and she feels like her voice is heard, then submission becomes a beautiful thing, not a dirty word. A prevalent problem in marriage, however, is that most men think that joint decision making and giving their wife a voice in decision making undermine their authority, but nothing could be further from the truth!

Matt Chandler wisely said, "I honestly lose all the little arguments [in my marriage] on purpose. Here's what I mean. If you look at Christian couples 90% of the time, on major issues, they come to consensus. They look at the Bible, they pray, they talk with one another, they might even seek wisdom from outside, they make the big decision together and it's great. 10% of the time, they can't come to consensus. Now the Scriptures say that when they can't come to consensus, the weight falls on the man to make the call... but I do not pick the music we listen to in the car, I do not pick the movies we go and see, I did not pick the car, I did not pick the couch we bought, I did not pick the colors of the wall, I did not pick the flooring we put down, I did not pick the house that we bought and on and on I could go. Now listen to me. I have strong opinions about everything. I have strong opinions about music, strong opinions about movies, strong opinions about style. My wife's and my opinions about how we decorate the home are in different universes. That doesn't change the fact that our house looks like a cottage. I've been urban my whole life and love urban and love modern. My workspace isn't even that. Somehow my workspace is like a cottage. I'm just waiting for a gnome to run out from beneath my desk. Ask her. I have never said, 'Could I have just this little space to decorate how I like it?' Never. I'll lose all of that. I'll go see *The Notebook*. Why? Because there's coming another day when I'm going to have to say, 'Okay, but we're going left. I do hear you, I do respect you and I do love you.' And my job in that moment is to lovingly lead her, and her job is to lovingly submit. I have just found it far easier to make that hard call when she wins everything else. We show our wives honor by cultivating their skills, talents and desires, and we show our wives honor by losing the silly fights."

We submit to Christ because it is the best life for us, and because we know that He has our best interest in mind. Your wife should have the same security in submitting to you as her husband. Now obviously we are human and you are going to mess up no matter how much you have your junk together. There is grace for that. You want the odds to be heavily in her favor to submit when you come to one of those decisions that you do not agree on. Because you've already proven you have her best interest in mind, she can trust that by following your lead it is going to be the best thing for her. That is when submission is no longer a duty. That is when submission is transformed into a delight.

The bottom line is this: give your wife a reason to want to submit to you. No one wants to be a friend to someone who is conceited and never thinks about other people, so how much less does a wife want to give herself and submit herself to a pompous, controlling, selfish jerk? Don't be that guy who pulls the "I am the head of this household" card because if you have to pull that card and actually say it, then you may think of yourself as the leader of your home but the reality is that no one is following. Christ earned the right, so to speak, to His special relationship to the church by leading her with selfless love, care and always with her best interest in mind. He was absolutely in charge but never flaunted His control or had to prove Himself. He led the disciples and continues to lead the church perfectly. *Could the same be said about the way you are leading and loving your wife?*

Turn to Appendix A for some questions to help you dig deeper into the content of this chapter

3

WHEN DEATH BECOMES HONORABLE, TRANSFORMATION IS SOON TO FOLLOW.

The Samurai Husband

Husbands, love your wives, just as Christ loved the church and gave himself up for her... -Ephesians 5:25, NIV

Picking out movies in my home is, well, interesting. I have learned that there are some movies I may really want to watch that are not even worth mentioning because I know before I can even finish the title the answer is already "no" because my wife is pretty anti-violence when it comes to movie selections. If there is even a hint of violence, there is no real point in asking. I just know to save those movies for a guy's night or when I am home alone. I know some of you can feel me on this because there are some movies that you just don't watch with your wife. Most women are not into action-adventure or movies whose premise is based on fighting. There are definitely exceptions, but for the most part, the ladies are into chick flicks and romantic comedies.

One movie that I distinctly remember watching (without my wife mind you) which fell into this category was *The Last Samurai,* starring Tom Cruise. It is the story of an extremely gifted military man who turned into a remorseful alcoholic, haunted by past mistakes and massacres he was a part of during the Civil War. Tom Cruise's character is eventually offered a job making an unprecedented amount of money to go to Japan to train the Japanese army to crush a perceived Samurai warrior rebellion. He is shipped to Japan, begins training, and during the first military engagement with the Samurai, Cruise is taken captive. He is brought back to the Samurai village as a captive and over the next few months he comes to know and love the way of the Samurai culture while simultaneously overcoming his alcoholism and nightmares of his traumatic past. When the time comes, Tom Cruise ends up casting his lot with the Samurais and fighting with them instead of against them, riding with the Samurai to engage the army he was paid to train.

The movie's final battle scene was comprised of 500 Samurai wielding swords, bows and arrows against a technologically advanced Japanese army well into the thousands. Even after creatively withstanding the first wave of the army's offensive attack and killing hundreds of Japanese soldiers, the remaining Samurai finally concede to the fact that defeat is inevitable against such a large, technologically advanced foe. They decide to make a final, fateful mounted assault directly into the heart of the remaining military stronghold knowing full well that no one will survive. Every last one of the Samurai warriors was mowed down by the superior firepower of the modernized Japanese army. The Samurai leader and hero, Katsumoto, mortally wounded by the gunfire, maintained his Samurai honor on the battlefield by committing seppuku, the Samurai ritual of maintaining one's honor through suicide, and therefore ending his own life to dramatically end the battle scene.

This movie piqued my interest in the Samurai lifestyle because of the way the Samurai were portrayed. While I obviously do not believe in the religious implications of the Samurai way of life and have no intention of killing myself in the name of honor, I still admire their discipline and commitment. Even the word Samurai means "to serve". The Samurai adhered to Bushido, a unique Japanese code of conduct that literally means "the way of the warrior". Bushido emphasized loyalty, honesty, obedience, and self-sacrifice among other virtuous qualities. These were a few of the tenets of Bushido that all Samurai abided by; they were kept with the utmost discipline. One such tenet was honor, a highly esteemed tenet of Bushido. Honor was so highly recognized that if a Samurai were to in some way lose his honor, the only way it could be regained was by committing *seppuku*, or the ritualized killing of oneself. For example, if a Samurai was faced with losing a battle, seppuku was the honorary custom to avoid falling into enemy hands and to avoid the shame of defeat. It was done by taking one's tanto, or short sword, and stabbing oneself in the stomach and moving the blade left to right and letting death overcome you silently. To keep the pain from becoming too great, a fellow Samurai warrior would eventually decapitate the disemboweled warrior. While this act may seem appalling to the Western way of thinking, seppuku was an honored tradition with the warrior class of the Samurai. This was one of the most respectful things a Samurai could do to maintain his honor.

Husbands, we have an even greater call and code than Bushido that we are called to follow. While the Bible never says to go kill yourself, the Bible does say to go kill yourself. Confused yet? Followers of Jesus don't literally plunge a blade into their stomach, but Paul calls us to be crucified with Christ so that we no longer live but Christ lives in us[8]. And Paul is merely echoing the call of Jesus to deny ourselves, pick up our cross, and follow Him daily,[9] putting to death our selfish and worldly wants and desires and allowing Jesus to be our greatest desire. In the same way that the Samurai honor their way of life by committing seppuku, followers of Jesus honor and glorify Jesus when they lay down their lives for Him. All throughout the New Testament we see this call to lay down our life. All throughout the New Testament, we are called to die to ourselves, to give up our rights and control, and to consider

8 Galatians 2:20
9 Luke 9:23

others better than ourselves.[10] It is not Bushido that Jesus' followers adhere to, but it's an even higher calling and one of the more important calls as a Christian; to give up control and relinquish one's life to Jesus.

This truth becomes very clear as Paul begins talking to husbands in Ephesians 5:25 and calls husbands to love their wives as Christ loved the church and gave Himself up for her. Now I hear a lot of people quote this verse, but most of the time it is a partial recitation. Most of the time you hear, "Husbands love your wife as Christ loved the church," and this is good, but it isn't Paul's complete thought. The critical six words in this sentence are *"and gave Himself up for her."* The reason it gets left out a lot of times is because it's the part that doesn't allow for much wiggle room as a husband. The reason it is so important not to leave out, however, is because it doesn't allow a lot of wiggle room for a husband.

Ephesians 5:25 calls husbands to love their wives as Christ loved the church and gave Himself up for her. As Christ GAVE HIMSELF UP FOR HER. Wow. Have you really ever thought of that? Have you allowed yourself to

---

10 Philippians 2:3-4

meditate on what it meant for Jesus to give Himself up for us? This is not an easy thing to set your mind on. Soldiers unmercifully beat Him and He took it. He was flogged with a whip made of nails, pieces of broken and serrated glass, and bone on its end so that it would literally tear the flesh off His back. He was then stripped down almost naked, surely after the blood had dried and adhered to His clothes, therefore reopening all of those terrible wounds. Soon after these wounds were reopened, the soldiers placed a massive piece of splintery wood on his bleeding back and shoulders and commanded Him to carry it to a hill called Golgotha, the place of the skull. Once He was painfully nailed to the cross and hoisted up, people came to see Him for the sole purpose of spitting in His face and unjustifiably mocking Him. Both Jews and Gentiles partook in the ridicule of the Messiah as He was being crucified for their sake.

Now would be a good time to put this book down, go rent *The Passion of the Christ* and watch that movie. It is the best visual aid that I know of to let you viscerally experience what Jesus went through on the cross. It was vicious. It was unjustified. It was horrible. Justice seemed nowhere to be found. The Innocent was being brutally murdered by the guilty. He was blameless and perfect in all aspects of the word but He was being assaulted as if He were the worst criminal in the land. The bottom line: Jesus did not deserve any of that. In fact, it was just the opposite. The people who deserved that horrific death were the same ones that were administering it to Him!

But Jesus not only endured it. He willfully, dare I say even joyfully[11], allowed Himself to be put in that situation. Even though He had all authority to do otherwise, to strike down the soldiers who were killing Him, to call down fire from heaven on those who mocked Him on the cross, to tell the earth to open up its mouth and swallow those who spit on Him in disbelief, He instead chose to look at them with compassion and say, "Father, forgive them, for they know not what they do."[12]

Husbands, love your wives, as Christ loved the church and gave Himself up for her...

What a high call to be a husband. As He gladly gave Himself up for the church, so you are called to gladly give yourself up for your wife. This is our act of worship and

---

11 Hebrews 12:2
12 Luke 23:34

obedience as husbands. This is our daily seppuku, the act of dying to yourself for the sake of Jesus and to love your wife with the love that He has for her.

The thing about Ephesians 5:25 is that it doesn't give us husbands an escape clause. If you're dead, you're dead. Jesus didn't partially die on the cross. He was completely *dead*. No pulse. No breathing. Nothing. Only after Christ totally gave Himself up in complete and utter submission to His Father did God breathe the resurrection life into His body. That is our example: to love your wife as Christ has loved the church and gave Himself up for her. So let me ask you a few pointed questions: "Have you truly died to yourself and your desires[13] when it comes to your marriage? When it comes to loving and serving your wife? What are you still trying to hold on to? Why?" (These are good questions that any good husband should ask himself.)

Back in Jesus' day when horses were used in battle, there was only one specific type of horse that was used. The type of horse has nothing to do with the breed or the skill of the horse. In fact, the horses chosen weren't always the best breed. The horses weren't always the fastest, the

---

13 Galatians 5:24

prettiest, or the strongest. Only one thing mattered when it came to a war-ready horse: the only thing that mattered was if the horse was broken. A horse had to be broken of its own will and own ways or else it was rendered useless in battle. When you are part of the cavalry's first offensive charge that is closing in on the enemy's front line of defense, their spears raised and pointed directly at you, you can't have a horse that is going to stop short or have any concern for its own well being. Have you ever seen any horses in *Braveheart, Gladiator,* or *Lord of the Rings* turn and run the other way? No way, because a horse like that would never be chosen to be ridden into battle. You need that horse to be fully submitted to its master and willing to do and go wherever he commands. I would rather take the mutt of the horse litter that is broken than some fast, strong, fancy horse that is going to turn the other way and get me stabbed in the back by my enemy!

Ephesians 5 is very clear what the Lord wants in a husband. A man that is broken. A man that is submitted. A man that is willing to give up everything for his master and his God. A man who is going to love his wife as Christ loved the church and gave Himself up for her. This is the kind of man God is looking for to lead his wife and family well.

No other type of man will do.

Expiation

Now I want to be very clear: brokenness does NOT equal weakness. That couldn't be farther from the truth. Jesus was physically abused and killed in one of the most wretched ways possible. His body was broken in the worst way possible... but that did not make Him weak. Jesus was not a pushover. He did not get crucified because He was too much of a weakling to speak up or stand up for Himself. On the contrary, there was purpose and cause for Him to receive what He endured. He was intentionally broken so that He, God Himself, could reconcile the ones He loved.[14] Because of His brokenness, we were given the opportunity to restore our relationship with God. God made Him who knew no sin to become sin for us so that in Him, we might become the righteousness of God![15] Jesus lived the perfect life we should have lived and then took our place and died the death we should have died. He became the proverbial whipping boy and was punished in our place *for the sins we committed*! That type of willful sacrifice and absorption of

---

14 2nd Corinthians 5:18
15 2nd Corinthians 5:21

sin takes insane resolve and strength and is far from any type of weakness.

This act that Jesus performed on the cross is actually called expiation. It's a theological term most of us haven't thought twice about before, but it is one of the wonders of the cross. This one word represents an important part of the power and beauty of what happened on the cross and why that was an eternally altering event in history. It is something that every husband should know inside out if he wants to actually love his wife as Christ loved the church. So, what is expiation and why does it matter to you as a husband? Well, keep reading...

Expiation is a huge part of what happen on the cross. Jesus took away our sin by taking it on Himself. The prefix *ex* means "out of" or "from," so expiation has to do with removing something or taking something away. In Biblical terms, it has to do with taking away guilt through the payment of a penalty or the offering of atonement. Jesus absorbed our sin and took it away so that we could be free from its penalty and effects. He didn't have to. He wasn't forced to. But He did, and therefore covered us because of His deep love for us. Because of this righteous act, we have the blemish and stain of sin removed!

Husbands, if we are to love our wives as Christ loved the church, then we need to regularly live out the act of expiation. What does that mean in the context of a marriage? It means that if your wife sins against you, yells in your face, doesn't do what she says she is going to, lets you down sexually, disagrees with you, or is being selfish, you take it like a man.

Take it like Jesus. Expiate the transgression.

Absorb it and don't fight back by pointing out her inconsistencies or by getting dragged into the fight. Simply diffuse the situation by absorbing the (fill in the blank): the rude comment, undone chore, cold shoulder, etc. Jesus covered us in our sin when we were proverbially spitting in His face, and we are called to do the same. He didn't call out all our shortcomings or fight back about why He was right and why we were wrong (even though that was and is always the case with Jesus). One way to flex your spiritual muscle as the head of the household is to follow His example; don't fight back and exert your dominance over your wife like the world tells you, but cover your wife in the same way Jesus covered you.

We need to redefine what it means to be a man, because this machismo garbage of the world doesn't hold a candle to Jesus. So take it like a real man; get used to practicing the art of expiation.

We look to Jesus as our example. As Jesus gave Himself on the cross, He never retaliated. He never justified His actions. He never called the people out on their sin. It wasn't because He was a coward. It wasn't because He was weak. He did the hardest thing possible to do when you know you are right and the other person is wrong... instead of proclaiming His rightness and proclaiming His victory, He loved them. He wasn't concerned about who was right or wrong, He was concerned about maintaining relationship with them. He was concerned about loving them. If there was ever a moment in all of history that someone could have been justified in defending himself, this was it!! The men who were spitting in Jesus' face and mocking Him while He was on the cross were the same men that Jesus was literally dying for. Jesus could have easily, and very justifiably, called down fire from heaven and licked those clowns up in righteous anger. But He didn't. Instead, He chose the high ground of expiation. He just took it in one of the greatest acts of love and strength this world has ever seen.

The ultimate act of seppuku.[16]

So I want you to ask yourself: Am I a Samurai Husband? When is the last time you, being rooted in love, just took it for the sake of your marriage? When is the last time you expiated a situation even though you knew your wife was wrong? If you never have, are you at least willing to try?

Gents, these are important questions! I cannot reiterate this enough: expiation is one of the most effective tools you have in your arsenal as a husband. It is like the bomb squad of your marriage that can effectively disarm massive blow-ups from occurring because the wires of the ticking time bomb of an argument are cut when you expiate a harsh word, a bad situation, or an emotional moment. Don't wait for the bomb to go off and simply resign yourself to be the janitor who has to clean up the mess after the explosion. Stop it from ever going off. Follow in the way of your Master.

---

16 Only it wasn't to preserve His honor; it was to guarantee ours!

The Struggle Is Real

When you utilize the art of spiritual seppuku and expiation, you are taking a very real stand against a very real enemy. And no, the enemy is not your wife. The Bible is very clear about two things: the first is that your marriage is one of the most important witnesses to God's grace, love, and glory that you will ever have the honor of being a part of.[17] The second is that our struggle is not really against flesh and blood[18]; we have a real enemy who is roaming around like a roaring lion looking for people to devour.[19] Every time you allow yourself to be overtaken by anger, every time you lash out in frustration, every time you have the opportunity to expiate but do not, you allow the enemy a foothold in your marriage. You allow the devil to take a small amount of ground in this ongoing battle for your marriage.

But remember this: every chance you have to love, to reconcile, to fight for your wife (even when it feels like she is the enemy!) is a chance to proclaim Christ's victory in you, your marriage, and makes you a participant in

---

17 Ephesians 5:25, 32
18 Ephesians 6:11
19 1st Peter 5:8

the grand scheme of God's promise that heaven is indeed invading earth.[20] What a cool thought: every time you love your wife well there is a shift in the spiritual realm where the armies of heaven are taking another step towards the utter domination of the enemy's camp. Every time you expiate a situation, forgive a harsh word, show love instead of reciprocating anger, you cry out with your actions that God is in control and this reality and truth ripple through your wife, children, your friends, and even your enemies in the spiritual realm. It may seem like a small thing in the moment, but over time, that one act of forgiveness turns into dozens of avoided arguments, which turns into hundreds of diffused attempts of the enemy's tactics, which turns into thousands of Kingdom victories, and your marriage is built up instead of broken down.

Jesus, let your Kingdom come!!

Turn to Appendix A for some questions to help you dig deeper into the content of this chapter

---

20 Matthew 6:10

4

THROWING THE SCORECARD OUT
THE WINDOW ONCE AND FOR ALL.

100/0

*Husbands, love your wives, just as Christ loved the church
and gave himself up for her... -Ephesians 5:25, NIV*

In 1962, Everett Rogers, a thirty-year-old assistant
professor of rural sociology at Ohio State University,
published the first edition of *The Diffusion of Innovations*,
a now widely popular and globally cited work in the social
sciences. In this work, Rogers proposed a theory that
sought to explain how, why, and at what rate new ideas

and technology spread throughout cultures. The crux of this groundbreaking thought was Rogers' Innovation/ Adoption Curve, which states that there are five types of adopters of new innovations and ideas:

1. *Innovators.* Innovators are comprised of 2.5% of the population that are the visionaries and greatest risk takers who tend to drive change.

2. *Early adopters.* This is the 13.5% that are the enthusiasts who embrace change and like to be among the first to try something new.

3. *Early majority.* The 34% that are the deliberate pragmatists who will adopt something if it is practical.

4. *Late majority.* This is the other 34% of the population who are skeptical of new ideas and only adopt if an idea or innovation is thoroughly proven.

5. *Laggards.* The final 16% of the population who are adverse to change and will often wait until they are forced to adopt.

Now I am kind of a nerd, so I get into random studies like this one. The problem is however, when I see a thing like the Rogers' adoption/innovation curve, something inside of me wants to be an innovator. I don't know what it is about my personality, but I always want to be the best. At everything. Even if I'm bad at it, I want to be better than everyone else. (I might have some issues that need to be dealt with.) It's a little ridiculous because even with 50-year-old social theories like this one, I want to be in the winner's circle! Maybe because it's reminiscent of high school and it touches on that adolescent desire to want to be like one of the cool (innovator) kids. Maybe it's because I want to win at everything and so when I see innovators on this scale I think, "Hey, they're the first!"

But if I am honest with myself, that just isn't me. I am not an innovator. The main reason why I am not is because I rely on tangible results. I would rather wait and see how the new technology fares for a little bit (early to late majority) and ensure it's a sure deal than to be that cool kid who has the newest gadget before anyone else. My logical approach to things also makes me slightly averse to risk taking. I'll admit it. It's not the coolest thing to say, but it's true.

This even bleeds over into my social life. I don't enjoy (at all) randomly opening up to a new person. I'm not and never have been the bubbly type who wears my heart on my sleeve or been a wild extrovert who will talk to anyone or anything. Before I dive in and put forth the effort, I want to make sure that a relationship is going to work. I am the quintessential social pragmatist. I want to make sure that I get out of a relationship what I want to get out of a relationship.

We all think this way if we are really honest.

This is why we are friends with some people, best friends with one or two, and not at all with others. We value the relationship, the things we have in common, and also enjoy the benefits that we receive from the people we are close to. If not, they don't become our friends. Period.

And here is where Rogers' Innovation/Adoption Curve plays into how men view relationships. Men are all early or late adopters, even laggards sometimes, when it comes to how we view relationships. We are, whether consciously or subconsciously, looking to see what we can get out of the relationships that we are a part of and we won't jump into one unless we think we will benefit from it. But this is also where a lot of us get into trouble as husbands; we treat our wives the same way we treat everyone else we are in relationship with. We want to follow the traditional social equation that will end up yielding the results we want and that are ultimately best for us: I want to know what and how much I have to do to get what *I* want out of this relationship. A lot of us look at marriage like a formula: if I do this, she'll do this, and then we are both happy (but more importantly, I am happy) with the results.

Let me give you a few examples that might bring this home. Not all of them are probably true for your family, but you'll get the idea:

- She wants romance. I want sex. If I am romantic, then she'll be in the mood and we have sex. Everyone wins, right?

- My responsibilities are mowing the lawn, taking out the trash, and taking care of the yard. Hers are cooking, laundry, taking the kids to sports practices, and getting them ready for school. If we both do our parts, everything is taken care of.

- I provide for the family financially, she takes care of the home. We do our part and it all gets taken care of.

But what happens when she isn't pulling her weight in your contractual agreement of who does what? What if you just pulled out all the stops on the romance side but later that evening your wife simply rolls over and goes to sleep? What if you bust your chops at work to provide for your family and you come home to a house that is so dirty and unkempt it looks like a bomb went off in it?

This is where most husbands find themselves more often than they would like to admit: in a cycle of unmet expectations (especially sexually), which leads to underlying frustrations about their marriage. We start to keep track of how much she is doing, or more specifically, how much she is *not* doing. We start to compare what we do and how we are pulling our weight and compare that to how she is not. The running tally has begun in our mind. And this is a dangerous place to be because once the tally gets started it begins to taint your view and causes you to always be looking through the lens of cynicism with everything related to your wife. You start to convince yourself that she is never going to meet the standard that you two agreed upon.

And you're right. She never will.

And herein lies the problem of the 50/50 approach to marriage. Basically, this type of approach to marriage says, "If you'll do your part, I'll do mine." But functionally what that means is "... but I won't do my part until I see you do yours." This kind of makes sense, right? Since there are two people in a relationship, it's okay to expect the other one to do his or her part in order for you to do yours. But this sort of thinking is actually quite damaging in a marriage, because it is human nature that we will not meet every single expectation someone has for us. We all fall short.[21] And nowhere is this more obvious than in your marriage.

This approach to relationships where we are looking to put in 50% and expecting the other person to put in the other 50% just isn't going to work. So what will?

Husbands, love your wife as Christ love the church and gave Himself up for her.[22]

Stop for a second and read that again. What do you see here in regards to percentages? Or more aptly put, how much did Christ give? You have to admit that there is a totality and finality when it comes to Christ's sacrifice for us. We do not see any sort of give and take approach to relationships here. We see an all-out-give-it-your-everything-even-if-it-kills-you type of mentality with Jesus. In Jesus' case, this is literally what happened. There was no 50/50 on his mind. It was all or nothing.

---

21 Romans 3:23
22 Ephesians 5:25

It was 100/0.

As a husband, I want you to take the idea of a 50/50 marriage out of your mind. Put it in a box somewhere to never be opened again. And then burn that box to ashes. Even if you are like me and you are not an innovator, an early adopter, or even an early majority type of person, this is the one place where that needs to change. And quickly. Your attitude should be the same as that of Christ Jesus[23] and you should just go on record as saying from here on out, you are going to give your wife 100% all the time *and expect nothing in return.* No questions asked.

What if she doesn't pull her weight? *You do it anyway.*[24]

What if she doesn't appreciate what you do? *You are not doing this for her praise, so it doesn't really matter.*[25]

What if I don't feel like it? *Do you think that Christ felt like dying on a cross? He clearly did not want to do it.*[26]

Not my will, but yours be done. These are the words of the God that we serve before His body was broken. This

---

23 Philippians 2:5-8
24 Mark 10:45
25 Colossians 3:23-24
26 Luke 22:42

is what we are to emulate. As Christ loved the church. He gave us 100% despite the fact that He knew many of the people He was doing this for would ultimately turn their backs on Him, spit in His face, mock Him, and scorn His sacrifice... so why did He do it in the first place?

To restore broken relationships. To woo humanity back to Himself. To be the "bigger man" who, although it was no fault of His own, made things right *at the expense of His own life.*

We all respect this type of sacrifice and love that someone shows, but we always like it from afar and when it is someone else doing it, don't we? This is the undying, fairy tale type of love that we read about but never really think exists. Well, think again. It is real... and you are called to live it out if you want to be a husband who is following in the footsteps of your Savior and answering the Biblical call to be a godly husband.

Contractual vs. Covenant Love

Now this is not something that is easy to do. Let's just clear the air on that right away. This doesn't happen overnight. This takes a deep understanding of God's love for you before you can properly live this out. You have to have been shown this love by God before you can emulate this love for your wife. If we have not experienced this from God, then we resort to what we know, and most of the relational currency these days comes in the form of contractual love. This is what we see in friendships, workplace relationships, and most of the time marriages, as well. It is the proverbial you-scratch-my-back-and-I-will-scratch-yours mentality. As long as our relationship is mutually beneficial, I'm in. But the moment that it does not benefit me, we are going to part and go our separate ways. It really does make sense on so many levels, so it should work in marriage, right?

This is an easy mentality to slip into.

On paper, this really does look compelling. *50/50 makes sense*, works in a lot of different relational settings, and seems to share the load of the marriage in a fair and responsible way. But within the context of a marriage, this line of thought starts to get muddy. Let's dig a little deeper and play this out from the husband's side of things.

In the contractual 50/50 paradigm, a husband may even start out joyfully serving his wife, but after a few years, the husband begins to question the commitment of his wife, especially if there is a season when she has begun waning a bit in her contractual responsibilities.

Let's throw out an example: baby #2 just came and the husband is waiting expectantly for that six-week post-baby sexual clearance from the doctor so he can reengage in the bedroom, but that six-week mark passes by and his wife is not showing any sign of sexual prowess or desire. Or his wife isn't as efficient or effective in her responsibilities around the home due to the burden of the second child. Or the kids are getting more attention than the husband is, and he feels slighted. (If you are a dad, I am almost 100% certain you have experienced one or all of these feelings at some time in your life.) Due to this frustration, the husband starts to slowly pull back on his contractual end of the bargain (he does less chores, he gives up on romance, his money and time start to go towards hobbies instead of his marriage and family, etc.). Because his needs aren't being met he stops doing his 50% of the contractual marriage agreement.

This ultimately leads to a lot of finger pointing and an endless stalemate. Instead of trying to fix the relationship, arguments arise with the sole intent of trying to prove to the other spouse why he/she is wrong and why all the problems in the marriage are the other person's fault.

Was this a fair transaction to begin with? You could definitely make a strong argument that it was, but this is where the contractual 50/50 approach to marriage starts to break down. Who is going to budge? Who makes the first move? What is fair in this situation and who can really say since both parties are so jaded and biased?

But we have to remember that "fair" is not our plumb line in this conversation. As husbands, our plumb line, our measuring stick, is *the Gospel*: nothing else and nothing less. I don't care what the newest self-help book says or the latest talking head or the foremost marriage expert says: if it does not line up with what the Bible says, then we, as followers of Jesus, disregard it. This is not a buffet where we get to choose what we believe, or a democracy where we have a vote. We don't get to pick and choose when and how we want to follow Jesus. When we don't like it we don't get to choose whatever pop culture tells us will make us feel better about our situation and ourselves. It simply doesn't work that way. Lordship means that Jesus calls the shots. Always. *Period.* Not a lot of wiggle room here, fellas. Discipleship and following Jesus will cost you everything[27], but you also gain everything that truly matters in the process.[28]

So if you want a marriage that is going to last; one that actually brings you the joy you have been looking for, then, as I have said before, you need to get this principle lodged into your spirit: 100/0. As a husband, regardless of what roles and responsibilities you have, you should do everything for your wife in regards to love and service and expect nothing in return. That is how Jesus loves us, so that is how we are called to love our wives. Your job, duty, and delight is to love your wife unconditionally and give her 100% of what you can bring and give to your relationship and not expect anything in return. And that is your Biblical call as a husband.

Now most men don't like this because it is "unfair". And they're right. *This is totally unfair.* This set up calls for you to utterly die to yourself in this relationship. And most Americans reading this book are going to get upset at this fact because we value and uphold fairness and equality as a God-given right in this country. I would go so far as to say that most Christians think fairness is a Biblical

27 Luke 14:25-33
28 Psalm 16:11

principle in some form or fashion. But when it comes to service and relationships, well, it isn't. Fairness is not a Biblical principle, it's not a fruit of the spirit, and it is not a command of Jesus. It is an American principle and a secular humanistic principle... but a Kingdom principle?

No.

If anything, as followers of Jesus, we are called to be massively lopsided and completely unfair! We should be the most unfair people on the planet. We should be so unfair that we are known for our unfair nature! In fact, do you know what another word for unfair is?

Grace.

Chew on that for a second. *Grace is not fair.*

Especially in marriage, we get ourselves in trouble when we live by the ridiculous notion that relationships are 50/50. If you are following Jesus, this is an absolute cop out. Grace means you give 100% when it is undeserved and you expect nothing in return.[29] Grace has to accompany the sacrifices and service you do for your wife or else it is simply dead works that you are going to use to leverage against her in the future for your benefit. I look at my marriage like

---

29 Ephesians 2:8-9

this: even if my wife Tracy never lifted another finger in our house, hated me forever, or God forbid became catatonic I would remain faithful to my wife because marriage is supposed to be a shining example of how Christ loved the church and never turned His back on us. Is this easy? Absolutely not. Is this Biblical? Absolutely yes.

That means regardless of what my wife does or does not do, whether she slaps me in the face daily or showers me with kisses, my call is to serve and love her with no expectation of getting anything in return. That is how Jesus loved me, so that is how I am called to love my wife. And what you find out is that as you are transformed into the image of your Creator[30], becoming more like Him in service and humility, there is a deeper satisfaction you receive when you are serving, which is much more fulfilling than the superficial happiness you experience when being served.

You might have the concern, "Well what if my wife doesn't submit to me or love me back even after I do all this for her?" If that is the case, then I am truly sorry, for that is not how it is supposed to be. But with as much

---

30 Colossians 3:10

love as I can muster, and please hear me on this, it doesn't change the fact that marriage isn't about your happiness; it is about your holiness and ultimately God's glory. In good and bad marriages, we have the opportunity to live out the Gospel. To love when it is difficult, to serve when we should be served, to show grace when it is not earned; that is the Gospel and you have the opportunity to walk it out in the context of a marriage more than in any other relationship you will ever have.

Marriage is death to self. Get used to it.

Unless a kernel of wheat falls to the ground and dies, it remains only one seed. But if it dies, it produces many seeds. This is when the fruit actually comes; post-death, and in our case, after we die to ourselves. The man who loves his life will lose it...[31] Jesus is a smart guy, and nowhere outside of salvation are His words truer than in marriage.

Guys this isn't easy, I will admit that. But nowhere will you be refined and come out holier and more like Christ than in your marriage, if you play your cards right and follow Jesus in His relentless pursuit of the ones He

---

31 John 12:24-25

loves. Nowhere will you find more joy and fulfillment then when you stop pointing fingers, when you stop waiting for her to do her part, when you stop holding things she did or did not do against her. You shake yourself free from the bondage and slavery that comes from holding onto grudges and unmet expectations.[32] I'm telling you, covenant love doesn't make sense on paper, just like Jesus dying didn't make sense to the disciples right away, and still doesn't make sense to an unbelieving world. But only in death can true resurrection take place. And only after resurrection can the true power of Jesus Christ be released in your marriage. Embrace the covenant that you entered into and do it the way God designed it; I guarantee that you will never make a better choice in your marriage than to take Jesus at His word:

Husbands, love your wife as Christ loved the church and gave Himself up for her.

Turn to Appendix A for some questions to help you dig deeper into the content of this chapter

---

32 Galatians 5:1

5

THE STRATEGY YOU NEED TO WIN THE FIGHT BEFORE IT EVEN BEGINS.

How to Fight Like A Samurai

Husbands, love your wives, just as Christ loved the church and gave himself up for her to make her holy, cleansing her by the washing with water through the word, and to present her to himself as a radiant church, without stain or wrinkle or any other blemish, but holy and blameless. – Ephesians 5:25-27, NIV

When I was 12 years old, before the movie *Fight Club* ever came out, I had my own little fight club with a few of my friends. We weren't natural scrappers so none of us had actually been in a real fight, but the thought of it was pretty enticing so we brought the fight to us. We even made a little boxing ring in my friend Alejandro's front yard so we could duke it out together. This was an ill-fated plan from the get-go because we didn't even have two pairs of real boxing gloves! One pair was a legit pair and the other pair was too small and didn't really have any padding left in them, but we didn't figure that out until after the first (and last) fight.

The fight was a match up between my friend, Drew and myself. To try to legitimize things, we had a referee and we each had a "trainer" in our corner to help us put our gloves on and give us advice before the fight. My trainer was my friend, Peter, another 12 year old who did not know a thing about fighting. Drew's trainer was Alejandro, the most athletic and largest one out of all of us, who always seemed to win at everything. I had no idea what I was doing and unfortunately for me, neither did Peter. His golden advice was to "just go crazy and try to hit Drew so many times that he can't even throw a punch back!" Alejandro on the other hand, told Drew, "Peter is probably going to tell Matt to come at your with everything he's got, so I want you to put your gloves up to cover your face so he can hit your body but can't hit your face. Let him give you a few body shots and when he starts getting tired, uppercut him as hard as you possibly can."

So the fight began and I came out swinging. I was landing blow after blow on Drew's body and near his face, so I was feeling like Muhammad Ali after a few minutes. I had complete ownership of the ring. Drew was scrunched into a little pathetic ball, cowering before the epic assault of my fists of fury. I started to get cocky and take larger blows and started getting my body behind some of the bigger punches. I finally wound up to deliver a punch with all my body weight when suddenly and seemingly out of nowhere Drew, for the first time, broke his defensive stance and gave me a punishing uppercut directly to the right side of my jaw.

As soon as his punch landed, my entire world went into slow motion. It was just like a movie; as soon as his glove made contact with my face, I spit out a huge wad of spit and blood, my head was thrown to the left as it followed the momentum of the punch, and eventually my body was forced by the trajectory of my head to follow suit. After spinning around 360 degrees, I froze up like a statue and fell to the ground without even an attempt to catch myself with my hands, face first in the grass. I got *knocked out*! (For the record, Drew had on the gloves with no padding... I still blame the knockout on that.) My friends laughed hysterically and our makeshift ref counted to ten to see if I was going to get up. My mind comprehended what was going on and heard the count, but my body was not responding. I thought I was pushing myself up but soon realized that I was actually just pressing my face harder into the ground. Up was down, down was up. The fight and the aftermath *completely* disoriented me. It took me the rest of the day to shake it off. I don't know which was worse: the shot to my face or the shot to my pride!

Now hopefully your wife has never knocked you out, but have you ever had a moment in your marriage when you get into a fight and it figuratively knocks you out and completely disorients your day? Have you ever left an argument that you can't stop thinking about and getting angry about all day? Or maybe it lasts even longer than that... have you ever been in a fight (or fights) that after awhile completely disorients *the trajectory of your marriage*? Your teammate suddenly becomes your opponent. Your closest ally is suddenly pitted against you as your enemy.

Unresolved fights and lingering arguments can unhinge even the strongest of marriages. Rarely is it a single knock-out, drag-out fight that kills a marriage. Most of the time it is the small disagreements left unchecked to fester that become the silent assassin for many couples. And husbands, I put the responsibility to keep this in check squarely on your shoulders. "Why?" you may ask. Because Biblically, we are not just called to be good role models for our kids or to placate our wives and simply keep them happy. We are called to be the conduits of Christ's supernatural transformation in our marriage and the agents of change in our homes as we walk in the power and the footsteps of Jesus.[33]

Yes, your wife plays a part in this too, but as you read Ephesians 5:25-27, there is a clear call for a husband to emulate Jesus by making his wife holy, to cleanse her, and to present her blameless in the same way that Jesus presented us to God in that way.

Is that a daunting task to anyone else??

I mean, blameless? *Is that even possible?!* Clearly, we do not absolve our wives from their sin in any eternal

---

33 Galatians 5:25

way; that is something only Jesus can do. But there are ways that we can absolve the sin of our wives and ourselves by creating an environment where the fights that do lead down the path of sin, disunity, discord, and destruction within our home don't even take place.

This chapter talks about what to do when the inevitable fight breaks out and how to crush the foothold that Satan will try to obtain if things go south during the process and aftermath of a fight. This is one of the major ways to ensure that your wife and marriage remains blameless, without stain or wrinkle or blemish... by snuffing out the attacks before they even have a chance to cause division and divisiveness that lead to a breakdown in your home.

So I'm going to teach you how to fight.

Learning How to Fight: Know Your Fighting Style

Even if you have never been in a fistfight, everyone knows that if you want to dominate an argument, take down a rival competitor, or even win a board game like Risk, you have to do your research. You have to know your opponent's strengths and their weaknesses and how to exploit them. You also need to know your own strengths and weaknesses in order to know how to mount an effective attack and win.

The same is true in a marriage, although you have to realize that the end goal is not defeating your wife; the end goal is to defeat your real enemy, the devil, who is trying to destroy your marriage every chance he has.[34] To do that, you need to know how to stop the strife and arguments in your marriage before they even happen and you need to have the tools to immediately diffuse them before things get out of control.

You can't do that, however, if you are completely unaware of your and your wife's fighting styles. So often my wife and I do marriage counseling where both the husband and wife we are talking to legitimately have the best intentions in their heart to make things right, but they always hit a wall when they actually try to talk with one another and work things out. Regardless of the initial resolve to make it work, an explosive argument ensues when they try to work it out together, no matter how hard they try to avoid it. And most of the time, it is because they are trying to tackle the problem in two radically different ways. Their way makes perfect sense to them, but their husband or wife "never seems to get what they are trying to

---

34 1ˢᵗ Peter 5:8

say", which leads to more strife, fighting, and frustration. Why do you think this pattern seems to repeat itself so often?

Husbands and wives don't know how to fight with one another because they lack the understanding of one another's fighting styles. It is like speaking two different languages and having no idea what the other is saying, which only exacerbates the problem! Husbands and wives have to know each other's fighting styles or else they won't know how to properly communicate in a way that their spouse can receive. This is such a critical first step which is, for the most part, overlooked!

So how do you find out your fighting style?

Just answer these two questions:

1. When you get angry, how do you respond?
2. What is your first, instinctual reaction when things get tense or heated?

Check off the following that apply to you:
- ☐ Do you shout and get loud?
- ☐ Do you shut down and go silent?
- ☐ Are you a crier?

☐ Are you a verbal jabber who says demeaning or hurtful things to your wife?

☐ Are you a problem solver who goes into problem-solving mode?

☐ Do you walk out of the room?

☐ Do you sweep it under the rug and pretend it didn't happen?

☐ Do you resolve things in an orderly and healthy fashion?

☐ Are you a get-it-all-out-on-the-table-right-now kind of guy?

☐ Do you need time to process and then circle back to the conversation in an hour or two?

These are a few ways that people will respond to conflict and a fight with their spouse. Take a second and think about how you deal with things. This is not an exhaustive list, so if nothing resonates with your style, then try to think of what does.

Now, take a second and think about how your wife responds. In fact, why don't you go ask her what she thinks your fighting style is and what hers is, as well, to make sure you are both on the same page.

Do your assumptions about each other's fighting styles line up? If so, you are off to a good start in diffusing future arguments. If not, well, this is part of the problem that you need to figure out!

This is important because fights usually linger and become toxic when either you or your wife (or both of you) feels like the other is not fighting fair. Maybe you are a get-it-out-on-the-table type of guy and your wife takes a longer time to process her thoughts. If you press her to resolve that conflict right then and there (thereby working through your fighting style and not hers), you may think things got resolved and feel good about the end result of the conversation. She, on the other hand, will remain a frustrated and angry wreck after your so-called resolution because she did not even get a chance to vocalize what her thoughts were on the situation. When this is the case, there really was no resolution. It becomes just one more scenario that Satan will try to weave into her negative and false train of thoughts that you don't really care what she thinks. (Don't give him that foothold!) [35]

---

35 Ephesians 4:26b-27

It may be the exact opposite in your home and you are the one who needs the time to process and your wife just wants to get the resolution over and done with. Or if you are loud and shout and she simply shuts down in response, then you may have dominated her and the conversation but you did not solve anything. I could go on and on because there are so many examples of how being unaware of your wife's fighting style causes a *permanent inability* to resolve conflict. When neither of you feels like the other understands what you are actually trying to say because one communicates in a wildly different way than how the other hears and processes, it is going to fail.

You have to know each other's style in order to effectively communicate with one another and resolve issues in a healthy manner. Otherwise, the more stubborn or dominant personality will "win" the argument while the other builds up resentment and anger because their voice is not being heard. This leads to hours, days, weeks, months, even years of pent-up resentment that will one day explode like a grenade in your face and in your marriage... and you will have never seen it coming.

When To Fight: Timing in Everything

I always find it interesting in movies when the president of the United States has to make the decision to launch nuclear warheads. Usually it is in the heat of battle or right before aliens attack... but even so, it is always quite a process. He has to pick up "the red phone" and make the decision and verbally confirm that he wants to launch the warheads. He then has a locked suitcase brought to him by a high-ranking military officer and the president has to open it with his retinal scan and fingerprints. Then he and the high-ranking military officer have to simultaneously insert their individual keys into the computer and count to three in order to turn them perfectly in sync to activate the system. Only after all this has happened can the president do what he set out to do 5 minutes beforehand when he picked up the red phone: he can finally hit the button to launch the nukes.

So why go through all the drama and such a lengthy process if he has already made up his mind and is going to simply follow through with his decision to launch the nukes anyway?

Because this is one of the most important decisions that a president can make. The process is to ensure there are safeguards in place so that this decision is not made lightly or flippantly. Launching nukes is no joke: the timing, situation, and environment have to all be in alignment or there will be globally catastrophic results!

If you are going to start World War III, you better be sure you are doing the right thing.

Now fighting with your spouse might not have the global implications of launching nuclear warheads, but sometimes a fight at the wrong time can feel like World War III in your home; you may even have the battle wounds to prove it. So ensuring the proper timing of the fight is just as critical as the fight itself, because the right thing at the wrong time is still the wrong thing.

For example, if it is late at night and you are still livid and your wife is about to blow a gasket if you say one more word... this is probably not the best time to hash it out. Just because there is tension in your relationship does not mean that it needs to get settled right then and there. Use some wisdom before you fight! There are many times when my wife Tracy and I disagree on something or something is said that sets me off or sets her off and you can feel the tension in the room. I mean, it is palpable. That doesn't, however, mean that we are going to fight right then and there and resolve it immediately. Many times, the way we approach a situation like this is by one of us asking the other a safe question like, "Are you okay?" or "Do we need to talk about this?" Clearly, we both know something is wrong, but this question allows us to have a conversation before *the* conversation. If we feel that this is not the time to talk it through, since the anger is still seething, the other will simply say, "I'm not ready to talk yet. Let's pray and talk about this in an hour."

We do this because it is much better to acknowledge there is a problem and agree that we are going to talk through this in 15 minutes, an hour, a few hours (depending on how heated or volatile things might get) than verbally lashing out at each other because neither of us have any control over our words or emotions at this moment in time. I would rather wait and talk later than unleash a slew of words that I am going to regret forever. (This takes massive self-control, but the benefits of exhibiting this key fruit of the Spirit[36] are so monumental you would be a fool not to wait.) If you just want to win an argument, then go ahead and talk when you are angry and be a machismo

---

36 Galatians 5:22-23

idiot and see how that works out for you in the long run. But if you want to actually serve and love your wife and help to present her blameless in this situation, then wait, get yourself under control, and don't say anything stupid in the heat of the moment. (If you want some more practical handles on this type of approach to fighting, check out Appendix B: The Green Zone)

A great question I frequently get asked at this point is, "So what happens between the time you agree to talk about it later and when you actually talk about it later?" And let me just be clear; it gets awkward, and I mean a-w-k-w-a-r-d in the Ulrich home during that in-between time. The tension is ripe. We don't really look at each other, we don't talk to each other for that time, and we usually go do separate things in separate rooms. If someone walked into our home at this point, they would probably take a look around, feel the tension, and then slowly back right out the front door because it would feel like there are two lions circling getting ready to pounce!

But timing is crucial, especially with fights. Allowing this time apart helps us to move out of irrational and emotional thinking and gives us time to filter our thoughts through the Holy Spirit rather than just through our hurt and aggression. Yes, you are probably angry at this point, and that's okay. The Bible never says being angry is a sin. The Bible does say, however, to not sin in your anger[37], and if you try to talk to your wife about a recent hot topic while you are angry, you are going to sin 99% of the time. So don't do it. Just don't. Allow yourself to actually cool off and start thinking rationally and in line with the Spirit before trying to resolve any issues with your wife.

Having this cool down time also allows us to pray and let the Lord do a lot of the work on our souls before we try to do that work on each other (which never works, by the way, because guess what? *You are not the Holy Spirit!*) The crazy thing is that I would say over 75% of the time, during that time of cooling off and prayer, I usually get convicted by the Holy Spirit that the entire root of the pending argument was because of something I did or because I was just being selfish! Once that realization hits and that conviction sets in, the fight in me dissipates. So instead of duking it out with one another, we end up apologizing before the fight even begins. Crazy right? That's what happens when we yield to the Holy Spirit!

---

37 Ephesians 4:26a

Timing is everything.

So now my wife and I have an agreement in our home that we will only fight when we are both ready. We have seen the fruit of waiting and experienced the conviction of the Lord before the fight began, and this has been a game changer for us! Bottom line: don't be dumb and fight when you are angry and emotional. Take a breather and give the Holy Spirit some time to do His thing and watch how a good amount of your fights are called off before you even get into the ring. This is just one of the very practical ways you move your wife and marriage into a posture and position of being blameless, and without stain and wrinkle.

Speak Her Language. Own Your Part.

Now there are definitely times when even after we separate, try to calm down and pray, that the point of contention is still bothering one of us. At this point, you need to address the issue and work it out. Don't let it fester and cause strife by not addressing the problem and letting the poison of that hurt settle in your soul. *How* you do this, however, is important! You need to approach your wife in a way that she is going to understand and receive. This means potentially moving out of your fighting style and into hers.

This is where you need to man up and serve her like Jesus would; in a way that she understands and can receive. If you are a get-it-on-the-table guy, you may need to wait a bit and let her process. If you are a sweep-it-under-the-rug type, this means stepping out of your comfort zone and bringing it up instead of waiting for her to do it. If you are a verbal jabber and have multiple opportunities to make her look foolish while she is saying her part, shut your mouth and let her talk. Love her in this way and you will reap the benefits of a tension and frustration free home. When you speak her language and show that you are trying to listen to her, even if it is not your natural way of doing things, she will respond positively. When your words *and actions* show that you are not trying to win the fight but are in it to see things reconciled, her defenses will come down.

Have you ever noticed that no one tries to pick a fight with a dead guy? No one goes into the morgue and starts talking smack to the dead bodies. Why? *Because there is no glory in fighting someone who doesn't fight back.* Winning actually means something when you overcome obstacles and a formidable foe. *Braveheart* would not be a legendary movie if William Wallace had not been such a massive underdog against a far superior English army.

David would not have the renown he did if he had been as old, as large, or as experienced a fighter as Goliath when he defeated him. Rocky Balboa gets hit so hard it gives him brain damage in the ring versus the Russian, Ivan Drago, in *Rocky IV*, but he comes back to knock out his Russian foe in dramatic fashion in the 15th round of their epic brawl. If Rocky had knocked him out in the first ten seconds of Round 1, that would have been a super lame ending to the movie, don't you agree?

The glory of victory comes because you overcome ardent opposition and defeat someone who is trying just as hard to defeat you. There is no glory, however, when the person you are fighting refuses to fight back, and this is amplified in the context of a marriage. Most of the time fights get nasty when you and your wife come ready to point out all the things that you think the other person did wrong. It simply becomes a verbal sparring match where you both just want to get things off your chest and prove the fault of the other party.

Imagine how different that conversation becomes when before your wife can even open her mouth to tell you all the things you did wrong, you begin by apologizing for all the things you did wrong and ask for her forgiveness. If you refuse to fight back and don't give your wife anything to push back against, the fight almost always immediately dies. That would change the direction of that conversation, don't you think?

Have you ever tried it? It is a very foreign concept when things start to get out of hand. I will admit, this is a hard pill to swallow and is not an easy move to master. It takes a lot of self-control and self-confidence to be able to check your ego like this. But if we really believe that it is Christ living within us[38] and that we are not doing this with our own power[39], then it is a doable feat.

Does this mean your wife doesn't need to take responsibility for what she did? No. Does this mean she just gets to have you grovel and apologize regardless of what happened every time there is a disagreement? Absolutely not. What this does mean, however, is that you show the way of humility and *lead her* in what the Christ-like response is supposed to look like.

Learn how to LEAD in your marriage, men! Don't just respond like a child. *Lead like Jesus.* Lead in a way that woos her into holiness. Then, when conflict does arise, she

---

38 Galatians 2:20
39 2 Peter 1:3

already knows your heart is for her and for reconciliation, not for pushing your agenda and winning. Lay down your rights[40] and reveal the way of the cross! Disrupt the fighting status quo with Kingdom tactics and allow Jesus to work in and through you as you change the spiritual climate of your home.

Forgive before you have to.[41]

Swallow your pride and own your part before she has to point it out to you.[42]

Adapt and engage her in her fighting style, not your own.[43]

Present her blameless, spotless and without blemish by stopping the fights from happening in the first place!

Turn to Appendix A for some questions to help
you dig deeper into the content of this chapter

---

40 Philippians 2:1-4
41 Colossians 3:13
42 Ephesians 4:2
43 1 Peter 3:8

6

TELL YOURSELF
THE RIGHT STORY.

<u>Believing The Best</u>

*He who loves his wife loves himself. In this same way,
husbands ought to love their wives as their own bodies. He
who loves his wife loves himself. After all, no one ever hated
his own body, but he feeds and cares for it, just as Christ
does the church— for we are members of his body. "For this
reason a man will leave his father and mother and be united
to his wife, and the two will become one flesh." –Ephesians
5:28-31*

Nothing is more unbearably annoying than bad drivers. There are times when I am driving in town with my two daughters in the car and I see someone speeding like crazy. The driver is speeding in the right lane, then rapidly accelerates and jerks the wheel left to try to get into that tight spot in front of the car in the left lane. He goes on to repeat this action with the cars ahead of me as far as I can see him. This grates my last nerve as a dad. I play out the scenarios of this reckless driver potentially hitting my car and hurting my kids because they are trying to impress their friends with their daring (and stupid) driving skills.

With that being said... have you ever had one of those mornings when everything goes wrong? You have the most important meeting of the year at work; you are making the pitch on the project you and your team have been working tirelessly on for the last five months. Your boss's boss flew in from corporate to hear your idea. The ramifications of this meeting could not be any greater in regards to the upward mobility in your career. This is the moment you have been waiting for!

So you set your alarm early to have some extra prep time for the day, but what you don't realize is that since you were resetting your regular alarm to a different time, you accidently set it at 5:30PM instead of 5:30AM. Your meeting starts at 8am sharp, but you accidentally sleep in until 7:25! You rush through your morning routine; shower, shave, get dressed, and dash out the door. The only issue is, it is now 7:45 and your commute is 15 minutes, which leaves you with absolutely no time to set up, debrief with your team, and get ready for this insanely important meeting you have at 8:00.

To make up for lost time, you push your mid sized sedan to its limits to try to shave a few minutes off your morning commute. The speed limit is merely a suggestion today. You weave in and out of traffic and get flustered when people don't get out of your way. You say things like, "Can't you see I am in a hurry!! GET OUT OF THE WAY!!" as you almost clip the front of the cars you are accelerating to pass. The light in the distance turns yellow, but instead of slowing down you speed up, because if you can make it half way through the yellow light, you won't feel as bad about the fact that you just blew right through it. You fly into the office's parking lot and sprint inside. You slide into the meeting at 7:59 and luckily you prepped your team well the week before and they had everything ready for you when you walked in the door. You take a deep breath, give your presentation, and it is a hit. At the end of the day your boss and his boss give you the "Atta boy!" that you were hoping to hear.

Now back to traffic: isn't it funny that when *you* are the high-speed driver weaving in and out of traffic you just expect everyone to know you only are doing that because you are in a hurry? Otherwise, of course you would not be driving like a maniac. This is a one-time deal! We say things to ourselves like, "Don't you know the only reason I would do this is because my job was on the line? Or because my kid was in the hospital? " You just assume that people should believe the best about your actions because, hey, you do have good intentions. And it legitimately was an emergency! So that in itself should justify your questionable driving, like a little bit of speeding, bobbing and weaving on your way to work for the most important meeting of your life, right?

But isn't it interesting that when it is someone else who is doing this, our tolerance level is non-existent. Is this not true? There is no benefit of the doubt for the driver who is going painfully slow, or the speedster who could have hurt my girls. We want everyone to give *us* the benefit of the doubt when we do something questionable, but when it comes down to it, we do not extend that same grace to those who are around us. Why?

Because you always believe the best about *yourself.* We rarely believe the best about anyone else. We judge ourselves by our motives, but we judge others by their actions.

And when it comes to marriage, this is an absolutely crucial concept that Paul addresses in Ephesians 5. He actually takes a lot of real estate in this section to drive this point home: *"He who loves his wife loves himself. In this same way, husbands ought to love their wives as their own bodies. He who loves his wife loves himself. After all, no one ever hated his own body, but he feeds and cares for it, just as Christ does the church— for we are members of his body."*[44]

What Story Are You Telling Yourself?

Paul understood that we always believe we have the best intentions when it comes to ourselves and that we always give ourselves the benefit of the doubt... but he also recognizes this is not the natural course of action within a marriage relationship. Why is this? Because life happens.

---

44 Ephesians 5:28-30

Fights happen. We get hurt by something our wife did or said and we start to hold grudges and start to keep a tally of the ways she wronged us (when we don't live by the 100/0 idea). And even though you started at the altar staring into your wife's eyes excitedly declaring, "For better or for worse," and thinking there was never going to be a "for worse" day in your marriage, you may have started to get jaded and cynical over time because things have not always gone the way you wanted.

And this is when the story begins.

You see, you are always telling yourself a story about your wife and your marriage. The story you tell yourself is made up of how you have filtered all the conversations, interactions, and non-verbal cues that have happened in your marriage up to this point. The story, however, is not just a history lesson. It also dictates how you are going to react or respond in future situations or circumstances.

These types of scenarios are critical moments and the story you are telling yourself matters. These may not seem like overly significant instances in your marriage, but it is the culmination of the dozens of these moments you have every week of your life that will define the story which determines how you view your wife and marriage. Let's break these down with some real life examples, shall we?

You can go two ways with the story you tell yourself in everyday scenarios: you can either believe the worst or believe the best about your wife in that moment and with your reaction. I'll give two examples to highlight what a difference it makes when your reaction is to either believe the best or believe the worst:

Scenario 1: You come home after an exhausting day at work and the kids are screaming and the house is trashed. What is your first thought when you step into that chaos?

Responding with believing the worst: You walk in and say under your breath, "What the heck have you been doing all day? Can't you at least keep the house clean and the kids from screaming?"

Responding with believing the best: You step into the house and think to yourself, "Man, it must have been as rough of a day here at home as mine was in the office. My wife looks exhausted. I bet she gave it her all today and still is feeling defeated."

Scenario 2: It's a Thursday night and you just had a nice dinner with your wife and you are feeling a little frisky, so you start to put the moves on her and she says,

"I'm really exhausted; not tonight. Maybe some other time." What's your gut reaction to her response?

Responding with believing the worst: She says, "Maybe some other time," and you take that as an instant rejection. You sulk and think of all your other guy friends who are having way more sex than you and you start to get frustrated at your sex life or lack thereof. You start to say things like, "She is just holding out to spite me," or, "Doesn't she know that I have needs too?" and start to feel sorry for yourself.

Responding with believing the best: After she says that, you think to yourself, "It must have been a rough day for her. Definitely looking forward to tomorrow night then!! I need to step up my romance game."

Do you see, regardless of even what your wife really meant, how your story and whether or not you believe the best about her radically alters your internal monologue and processing? And this is key: it not only affects you, but it also affects what is going to happen during the subsequent interactions you will have with your wife. If you are constantly thinking she is useless around the house, she will pick up on that and it will cause fights. Or if you start to pout about your lack of sex life, let's just be honest: that really isn't going to help anyone. I have never heard a wife say, "My husband is sulking about our lack of sex life, and that just put me into sexual frenzy!" Never. You just need to accept the fact that it is not about you and that it is not happening tonight. When your wife sees that you are content, not just after the sex but really after her well-being, that you continue to be romantic, help around the house, and do the things good husbands do... now that is how you are going to turn your wife on and get her in the mood!

But this starts with that initial response and the story you are telling yourself. Now I can hear some of you reading this saying, "But what if she is useless around the house?! What if she never wants to have sex?!" Then you have a deeper issue that you need to address. (Sex is never about sex with women, by the way, so find out what is really going on underneath that lack of intimacy.) Serve your wife by loving and helping her figure things out. Take the lead on things; don't just wait for your wife to solve the problems. Talk it through and discover what the root problem is together at your suggestion. Sacrificially meet her needs and she will meet yours. But even if she doesn't, that is what you signed up for. Not to become happy, but to become holy and represent Christ and the unbelievable love He has for His church. And the irony is that exemplifying this is what is going to reignite the connection between the two of you! Do you see the genius of Christ in these situations and how Ephesians 5, even though it seems totally not about you, will actually benefit you in the end?!

I do not want to discount the fact that life and marriage can get hard. And lonely. And bitter. These things happen; I get that. And for that, I am truly sorry. It is not supposed to be like that. Or if the story you are telling yourself is somewhat based on factual circumstances like:

Your wife isn't the same fun-loving girl she was when you got married.

She has become a nag over the years and all she does is remind you of all the things you do wrong.

She doesn't respect you as a husband the way she used to.

Fill in the blank with whatever has happened in your marriage over the years that has taken you from the utopic glass-is-always-full viewpoint you started your marriage with to where you may be now. But it is not going to get better by you telling yourself the same old story of how she is this way or that way or how she does these things just to spite you. You have to make the shift in your spirit and mind and tell yourself, "I am going to believe the best and the change is going to start with me."

You need to 1 Corinthians 13 your wife, because true love keeps no record of wrongs.[45] If you wipe the slate clean, you will free yourself from the baggage of the negative story you have been telling yourself and you will have the chance and ability to start over and make things new. Is this easy? By no means. Is it worth it? It's worth every ounce of energy you put into it. To have a marriage that is healthy and whole and representing the love of Christ is one of the most fulfilling things we were created to reflect and be a part of. When we really believe the best about our spouse and start thinking about her the way we think about ourselves and start serving her the way we would want to be served, then the game changes. And it drastically changes for the better.

Turn to Appendix A for some questions to help you dig deeper into the content of this chapter

---

45 1 Corinthians 13:5

7

THERE IS ONLY ONE MASTER, AND TRUST ME, IT IS NOT YOU.

The Samurai Master

For this reason a man will leave his father and mother and be united to his wife, and the two will become one flesh." This is a profound mystery—but I am talking about Christ and the church. However, each one of you also must love his wife as he loves himself, and the wife must respect her husband.
–Ephesians 5:32-33

Have you ever been white water rafting? Some of the most dangerous rapids form when two rivers, which may have flowed pretty smoothly on their own, merge. When they come together they often create something quite turbulent. Why? Because each river has its own current that is going its own way and when those two currents collide with each other, it produces powerful undercurrents and harsh rapids. As the rivers flow downstream, however, the collision of those currents subsides. The result of this becomes the emergence of a new river that is broader, deeper, and more powerful than either of the two rivers were on their own.

The same is true of a marriage relationship. If you are/were like most newlyweds, you probably experienced some rough waters in the beginning of your marriage. It's not easy reforming habits you have had all your life. Going from looking out for one person to trying to merge two totally different people's habits and preferences can be really tough. But as the currents of your two lives merge, the two come together to form something altogether different, which is broader, deeper, and more powerful than either of your two lives on their own. The two truly become one.

We as husbands have to realize that there is no longer "you vs. her" anymore. It is not your current and her current; it is our current. It is now ours, so there is no real winner if there is disagreement or discord! We both lose when do not act in unity and with the best interest in mind for each other. It is our loss when either one of us start telling himself/herself the wrong story. We both lose when we fight because even if one wins, the other loses and if you are one, that means we both lose.

There is a new level of relationship dynamics that comes when we get married and become one. This is the profound mystery that Paul speaks of in verses 31 and 32. We don't literally become one person, but there is a deep connection physically, mentally, emotionally, and spiritually that happens which is unlike anything else we will ever experience here on earth. The depth and level of intimacy in this relationship is absolutely unique. I can without a shadow of a doubt say that the absolute best moments of my life have been with my wife. The darkest and most despairing moments of my/our lives we experienced together. The most intimate parts of my soul that no other human being on this planet has seen or experienced have been seen and experienced by her. The profundity of our relationship is unlike any other.

And husbands, this is the type of relationship and intimacy the Lord is looking to share with you. This is the model and the experiential example we receive to illustrate how Christ loves His church and His people. Marriage is one of the glorious ways you and your wife are to viscerally and pragmatically mirror and experience the love, depth, and intimacy of your relationship with God.

As the husband, you are tasked with leading yourself and your wife in this beautiful and wholly other spiritual experience.

Daunting, isn't it?

And the bad news is *you can't do this well.* You don't have the strength. You don't have the wisdom. You don't have the discipline. Sorry guys, you just don't have what it takes.

But Jesus does.

The *only* way we can be the husband that we are called to be is to acknowledge that we don't have what it takes and to remain close to the source of our strength. We need to abide in Jesus and allow Him to fill us with the vision, supernatural power, forgiveness, peace, self-control, and all the other things we need to make it in marriage. Apart from Him, you can't do anything. [46] But there is a counter-intuitive truth that is only found in the Kingdom of God which states that those who truly have strength are the ones who proclaim freely that they are weak and are desperately aware of their need for supernatural assistance.[47]

Matthew 5:3 in the Message translation says, "You're blessed when you are at the end of your rope. With less of you there is more of God and His rule." Have you ever felt like you were at the end of your rope in your marriage? That you have tried everything you could think of and nothing really worked? That you gave it your everything, but that still didn't seem like enough? Good. If you answered yes to any of these questions, then you are probably now prepped and ready for God to take over. But you have to give it up to Him. This is part of the mystery of the Kingdom: the less you try to rule and lead out of your own strength, the greater the leader and husband you will be. Period.

Let go and let the Lord do His thing. Submit yourself to the Samurai Master.

---

46 John 15:1-8
47 Isaiah 40:29

Long Devotion in the Same Direction

I want to revisit the thought of the warhorse in Chapter 3. Do you remember the only trait that really mattered for a successful warhorse? That's right, it was *brokenness*. Some of the strongest and fastest horses never saw the battle lines because they could not be broken, thus rendering them useless to their rider.

If you think that you can be a godly husband and do it without being broken, then you are in for a rude awakening, my friend. You may even be a great husband in your own power, but there is no way to execute Ephesians 5 without utter brokenness leading you to a radical dependence on Jesus. As husbands, we have to do what many of us have tried to steer clear of for years. It goes against everything the world tells us about being a man and having all your junk together and being strong. If we want to do this right and if we want to do this Biblically, we have to recognize our weakness, humble ourselves, and break before the Lord. Only after we swallow our pride[48] and we acknowledge that we do not have what it takes to do this right can the Lord really use us with the positional authority that He had in

---

48 James 4:10

mind for a husband who will lead his wife well. Much like the body of a very capable Savior was broken for us, we must break under the Lordship of Jesus Christ in order to be all that God has created us to be as husbands.

What does this mean to be broken? It means that you live your life with the same mentality Jesus had: "Not my will, but yours be done,"[49] regardless of the cost. It means that your pride and your desire for control are extinguished and put to death... not just so you can roll over and die, but because a seed must fall to the ground and die if there is any hope for fruit to be produced from it.[50] In the same way, you need to die to your selfish ambition and desires so that out of your death to self can the power of the resurrection fully take place in your life and marriage.

This is not easy, but this is the call to all followers of Jesus, particularly husbands. This is not an overnight transformation, however. This is a long devotion in the same direction. You are not going to become a perfect husband overnight, much like you don't become a perfect follower of Jesus overnight. There is a process of sanctification that leads to godliness. In the same way, you

---

49 Luke 22:42
50 John 12:24

start with an open heart to the Lord to change you and you go from there. Take it one day and one thing at a time. Ask the Lord to break you and build you back up in His resurrection power. Ask him for eyes to see your wife, your marriage, and your home with His love and compassion. Take time to create practical handles, whatever that may look like in your marriage. Brush your wife's hair, change your baby's diapers, do dishes, clean without being asked, take your wife out and actually listen and engage with what she has to say, take her hands every night before you go to bed and lead her in prayer, say "I love you" five times a day. Whatever your wife needs, meet that need in and through the love of Jesus, because let's face it, you can't do it on your own.

The Way of the Samurai Husband

One of the most heart-felt prayers of my life is to raise my two daughters in a godly and Christ-centered home that leads them to a deep and rich love for Jesus. I desire for them to experience the tangible love of God. I long for them to have first-hand encounters with Jesus that they cannot deny. I truly want them to taste and see the Lord is good. I want everything to line up so they see the beauty of our Savior and get radically transformed by His love.

But above all, I want my girls to see the way I love their mother, the way that I serve her, the way that I sacrifice for her, the way that I dote on her, the way that I look at her, the way that I would do anything for her. I want them to see all of that, and I want them to say to themselves, "If how Daddy loves Mommy is the way that Jesus loves me, then I want everything Jesus has for me."

As a husband, you have a decision to make. This decision will not only affect your marriage, but also your wife, kids, neighbors, coworkers, and even random people who you come in contact with. In fact, this may even have eternal ramifications. It may well be the cornerstone of your life's evangelism and the way you give a world whose ears are deaf to the Gospel the first sound of eternity they can hear.

The decision you need to make is whether or not you are willing to step into the ageless calling to lead your wife well. To love her as Christ loved the church and gave Himself up for her. To sacrificially serve, love, and honor your wife in a way that embodies the leadership, the humility, the power and the grace of Christ Jesus.

It will be your rendition of the Samurai seppuku, the volitional death to yourself. It is a high calling that will cost you your life, but one worth giving yourself to because in this death is the only place where you will actually find new life. Whoever tries to keep their life will lose it and whoever loses their life will preserve it.[51] In the same way, a husband who tries to keep control will lose it, but whoever turns it over to Jesus will preserve it. So it's time for you to make the choice and draw a line in the sand. Ask yourself what type of husband you want to be. It's time for you to ask yourself what kind of legacy you want to leave for your wife and your family.

It's time for you to embrace the way of the cross.

It's time for you to embrace the way of the Samurai Husband.

Turn to Appendix A for some questions to help
you dig deeper into the content of this chapter

---

51 Luke 17:33

Appendix A

Samurai Husband Study Guide

We Are Better Together.

The Christian life was never meant to be lived alone. We are communal beings made in the image of a triune God and because of that, we thrive in community. We flourish and grow when we are together. The greatest gains you will make are when you run after Jesus *with others*.

Becoming a godly husband is no different. We may think that our marriage is personal, and it is, but that does not mean there cannot be growth when other godly men are invited to help journey with us in our pursuit of Jesus in the context of our marriage. There is an exponential increase in our ability to make spiritual gains when we find other husbands with the same goal in mind.

Form a Samurai Group.

The best way to maximize this study is to gather a few husbands (or husbands-to-be) that you can help disciple, or that can help disciple you, and start a 7-week "Samurai Group." Band together with them and commit to reading one chapter and discussing these questions together each week. Be real and raw with where you are in your marriage and how you want to grow, and then watch how God will transform you, as an individual and as a husband, through the content and the camaraderie of a group like this!

Go Deep!

These discussion questions are meant to help you dive deeper into the content of each chapter. They are not intended to be answered with short, one-word or one-sentence answers. They were created to really drive home the theological and practical points described in each chapter. So don't hold back. Get real with one another. Get raw and share what is really going on in your marriage, heart, and mind. When asked about how you are going to apply this to your marriage, really give it some thought, instead of just spouting out some generic answer. The more honest and open you are with the Lord and with other men, the more growth you are going to see.

Chapter 1: From Happy to Holy to Glory

- Before reading this chapter, what would you have said the main purpose of marriage is? Why would you have said that?

- How has your view changed since reading this first chapter?

- "Marriage is not about your happiness. It is about your holiness." How does marriage make you holy?

- Give some examples of how Jesus functioned as a servant King while He was here on earth. Why was His posture and voluntary position as a servant King so revolutionary?

- Give some specific ways of how is marriage supposed to reflect the relationship between Christ and His church.

- List three things you can do right now that would give God glory if you made the shift from focusing on your happiness to focusing on holiness in your marriage.

Chapter 2: S#*%it

- What do you interpret the idea of Biblical submission to be and what does it look like day-to-day?

- How do you balance the tension between leadership and submission? Do you feel the call to "submit to one another" equates to weakness or takes away from your leadership as a husband? Why or why not?

- Can you honestly say that your wife submitting to you is the best thing for her? Why or why not?

- Is there anything in your life (sports, hobbies, work, etc.) that your wife is competing with in regards to your affection?

- Does your wife know that she is your top priority? If so, how does she know that?

- What are some ways you can put a point on the board with your wife? What are the ways you can love her well day-to-day?

Chapter 3: The Samurai Husband

- In what ways does God call us to die to ourselves on a daily basis? Give some very practical examples of how this plays out (or should play out) in your life.

- Have you truly died to yourself and your desires when it comes to your marriage? When it comes to loving and serving your wife?

  ◊ What are you still trying to hold on to? Why do you think that is?

- What does it mean to be broken before God as a Christian? As a husband?

- In your own words, explain what expiation is.

- What are some ways that you can apply this concept of expiation to your marriage this week?

- Have you even thought of your marriage as being under attack from the devil and that every time you don't give into a selfish temptation you are bringing heaven to earth?

  ◊ Does this change your perspective on your marriage? How?

Chapter 4: 100/0

- Where in your marriage are you functioning in a contractual 50/50 type of contractual agreement?
- How can you start shifting into the 100/0 mentality?
    - ◊ Give some specific examples of how this will play out in your marriage.
- How can you guard against the feeling that you are doing everything and she is doing nothing if you adopt this 100/0 mentality?
- Describe the major differences between viewing marriage as a contract versus a covenant.
- How often does the idea of fairness play into your marriage? Give some examples of how this idea of being fair plays out in your home.
- How would our relationship with Jesus play out if He based things on what was fair and unfair?

Chapter 5: How to Fight Like a Samurai

- What is your fighting style? Take some time to actually answer the questions found in chapter 5:
  - ◊ When you get angry, how do you respond?
  - ◊ What is your first, instinctual reaction when things get tense or heated?
- What is your wife's fighting style?
- When you compare the two, do you both have similar fighting styles, or are they totally different?
- What can you do to ensure that you can fight in a way that both of you understand one another?
- Based on past fights, when would be the best time for you to engage in conversation? Immediately? After waiting a little bit of time? Form a plan of action that includes *when* the best time to fight would be.
- What are some ways that you could be "the dead guy" in the fight? How could you stop the fight from even starting with your wife in this regard?
- Read Appendix B and try practicing "I" language this week with your wife.

Chapter 6: Believing the Best

- How are you believing the best about your wife?

- If you are honest, how are you *not* believing the best about your wife?

- How would you sum up the story you are telling yourself about your wife?

  ◊ Do you like where that story is and where it is heading? Why or why not?

- Are there areas of your life where it is easier to tell yourself a better story than others? Why do you think that is?

- Do you feel like you are abiding with Jesus and spending time with Him regularly in a way that allows you to lead your wife the way Jesus leads you? Explain.

- Describe what type of legacy you want to leave as a husband. Write it out and share it with your wife and your Samurai Husband Group and let the men in your group hold you accountable to be the man and the husband God is calling you to be.

Chapter 7: The Samurai Master

- Give five practical examples of how your relationship with your wife should emulate the way that Christ loves the church.

- Is it hard for you to acknowledge that you don't have what it takes to be a godly husband? Why or why not?

- List a few ways that you have allowed Jesus to give you strength to be the husband that He is calling you to be.

- List a few ways that you still need Jesus to give you strength to be the husband that He is calling you to be. Why do you think that these aspects of marriage are hard for you to relinquish control to Christ?

- Have you ever thought of your marriage as being part of your evangelism to those around you? Does this change your perspective on marriage? Why or why not?

- How can you start or maintain the long devotion in the same direction of being a godly, Samurai husband without losing steam a few months from now? What are some ways you can keep that momentum going for the long haul?

Appendix B

THE MOST CRITICAL BATTLE TACTIC YOU NEED TO KNOW.

The Green Zone

Ever had something that you needed to tell your spouse but you know that if you do, it is pretty much a 100% chance that an argument will break out? How do you fight fair? How do you get to the root of the issue without having an all-out brawl? What do you do when there is clearly a misunderstanding but it is a sensitive subject that you know is going to bring up some emotions and a potentially heated argument? You enter into what my wife and I call "the green zone."

The green zone is a saying we use when we are about to bring up an emotional, tension-filled comment that has a high probability of being misinterpreted and leading straight into a fight. Here are the steps for getting to the green zone and then what to do once you get there:

Step 1: Pray and Expiate.

If Tracy (my wife) did something that offended me, the first thing I do is try to expiate that comment or action (see Chapter 3 for a refresher on expiation). Usually after I pray through something that offended me, more often than not the Lord shows me that the reason I am upset is more because of my pride and selfishness than anything else. This is always a good way to end a potential argument; before it begins.

Step 2: 24 Hour Holding Period.

If it is something that I try praying through and I still have angst, hurt, or concern about the comment or situation, my next step is to WAIT 24 hours before I bring it up. "Why so long?" you may ask. Because a lot of times, I need multiple prayer sessions and time to cool down to make sure I am not approaching my wife while I am in an emotionally fragile or wounded place. Arguing when you are emotionally upset is just plain foolish. No one wins in that situation. You both say things you wish you hadn't and the situation ends up being worse than before. The 24-hour wait ensures that your temper and emotions are level and it gives Jesus a shot to show you if the problem is really you or the way you interpreted what your spouse said. If it is something smaller, shorten the timeframe, but use wisdom and don't fool yourself into entering into the conversation too early, especially if you just want to "get it off your chest."

Step 3: Entering the Green Zone.

If it can't be expiated and after 24 hours I still feel like I need to talk it out, then now it is time to enter the green zone. The green zone is aptly named because it is a place that is safe to communicate without fear of retaliation and/or arguing. The way it works is that if your spouse comes to you and says, "Hey, we need to talk. Green zone," then that is your cue that she is trying to say something to you in love without arguing. Respect that. So when your spouse pulls that card, you have to collect yourself, probably sit down, and just listen. That's it. Listen to what they say.

Part of the rules of engagement is that you are not allowed to talk back, defend yourself, or attack. You have to receive and simply take it.

Even if you think she is wrong. You are only allowed to listen.

Here's why: This gives your spouse a safe place to not attack you, but to express how she feels. By not allowing yourself to fight back, you keep it from escalating in the emotion of the moment. Tracy and I simply say if we are at the receiving end, "Thanks for letting me know. I will work on that." And that's it.

Step 4: Repeat Steps 1 & 2.

From here, if you are on the receiving end of a green zone talk, it is now your turn to take that to prayer, ask the Lord to show you what you need to work on, and expiate the things that can be expiated. Most of the time, the problem gets solved before the argument occurs, because both spouses are trying to work on themselves. But if there are still unresolved issues, then repeat the green zone process. If you get to a third green zone attempt, then it is time to enter into a conversation with one another.

The beauty is that by the time you have that conversation, you already have at least two days of prayerful contemplation of how you can improve the situation by improving yourself. And hopefully by this time, you already know what you need to do.

Here are some other tested and true fighting tips that may help you in your marriage that are tested and true:

Think with your spirit, not with your emotions.

It is easy to think with your emotions when you feel attacked, defensive, or put down. Our instant reaction is to react in kind when emotions are dictating our thought process. Thinking with your spirit, however, means that instead of filtering your thoughts through your emotions, you train yourself to filter things through the spirit. Go through the fruit of the spirit (Galatians 5:22-23) or Paul's exhortation to have a holy thought life (Philippians 4:8) and see if what you are about to say makes the cut with those standards and parameters. If you don't know those passages by heart, it might be a good time to memorize them. By filtering your thoughts through the Spirit and the Word, you stand a much better chance of not sticking your foot in your mouth.

Use "I" language.

One thing that goes a long way is not what you say but *how* you say it. Check out these two examples:

1. "You always say demeaning things and I am tired of it. You need to stop being so sharp with your words!"

2. "When we really get heated, I feel belittled when sharp words are used."

3. "You shouldn't have spent that money on another new dress and shoes when money is so tight. You are being selfish."

4. "When I saw the clothing purchases on our credit card, I felt anxious and angry because we are on a tight budget. I think we need to talk through the budget again."

Do you see the difference? One is attacking and the other is focused on how you feel, not on your spouse's shortcomings. The reason this is so important is that you get the same point across but it doesn't put your spouse on the defensive. It is a way to talk that helps you get into more of a green zone type of conversation. The more you can take fighting words out of the equation, the better the chances you aren't going to fight. Using "I language" is a huge help in this area.

Set the tone.

Let me restate something; it is not what you say but *how* you say it. In this case, I am talking about the tone of your voice. You can say, "I'm sorry," or even, "I love you," and it does more harm than good because of the way you say it. This is why it's important to ensure you aren't talking with your emotions; you will get yourself in trouble. When you say the right things, make sure your heart backs up your words because that comes out in your tone. Focus on how it comes out, not just the words you are saying. Especially husbands... your wife has a PhD in hearing what you are really saying, even though your words may be saying something else. Mean what you say and let your tone back it up.

Appendix C

GIVING YOU THE HANDLES YOU NEED
TO ACTUALLY MAKE THIS HAPPEN.

The Daily Life of a Samurai

If you are like most guys, then you need some handles. Practical handles. So here are 50 ways to intentionally and sacrificially love your wife on a daily basis. The way of the Samurai Husband is a long devotion in the same direction; so don't just read the book. Put it into practice *every day*. Below are some good places to start or to build up your repertoire:

1. Tell your wife you love her every day.

2. Do the dishes without being asked.

3. Kiss her when you leave the house for work.

4. Give her a back massage or physical affection that doesn't lead to sex.

5. Change your kid's diaper before she has to ask you.

6. Brush her hair.

7. Leave her a surprise note that says something meaningful.

8. Stay off your phone and email when you get home and be fully there when you are with her.

9. Let her sleep in on the weekends while you take the kids.

10. Hold her hand when you are in public.

11. Call her during the day for no reason other than to ask her how her day has been.

12. Lead your family in devotions throughout the week.

13. Bring her home flowers just because.

14. Compliment something you love about her body regularly.

15. Compliment something about her that has nothing to do with her body even more regularly.

16. Make her coffee in the morning before she gets up.

17. Lay your hands on her and pray over her and your family daily.

18. Bring home her favorite take out or treat.

19. Pack the kids' lunch for school.

20. Clean the bathrooms.

21. Plan dinner and make it.

22. Turn off the game or the TV and spend time together instead.

23. Give her a day or an evening off while you watch the kids and let her do whatever she wants.

24. Show interest in the things that she is interested in (even if you are not interested at all).

25. Plan a date night without her knowing.

26. Encourage her in front of others.

27. Encourage her when she is not there.

28. Open the door for her.

29. Get the kids ready for school in the morning.

30. Make it a point to read the Bible regularly with her/the family.

31. Ask her what you can help her with that day.

32. Bring coffee or breakfast to her work (or back home if she is a stay-at-home mom).

33. Break the routine and do something unexpected for her.

34. Tell her how beautiful she is.

35. Sneak a love note in her purse before she goes out.

36. Genuinely listen to her when she tells you about her day.

37. Put the toilet seat down.

38. Throw your dirty clothes in the hamper.

39. Take the initiative and run the errands for her.

40. Say thank you often and maintain a posture of gratitude.

41. Be the one who secures the childcare for your date night.

42. Watch a movie that *she* wants to watch.

43. Listen for the things she wants but doesn't really need (books, a snack, small things) and get them for her without it being a special occasion.

44. Own bath time with the kids.

45. Take care of her car (make sure it is full of gas, do the oil changes, etc.).

46. Rub her feet after a long day.

47. Surprise her by planning a girls night out for her with her friends.

48. Put some music on in the background and spontaneously dance with her at home.

49. Be the one who takes the lead when it comes to going to church.

50. Because it deserves reiteration I'll end where we began: tell her often how much you love her.

THE SAMURAI HUSBAND

BECOME THE **HUSBAND/COUPLE** GOD CALLED YOU TO BE

For more information, tools, and resources check out:

@MRULRICH

@MRULRICH

@SAMURAIHUSBAND

WWW.SAMURAIHUSBAND.COM

Made in the USA
Columbia, SC
17 October 2017